MARRIAGE RECORDS OF BRUNSWICK COUNTY, VIRGINIA, 1730-1852

I0027327

Compiled By

AUGUSTA B. FOTHERGILL

With an Improved Index by
Anita Comtois

CLEARFIELD

Originally Published 1953

Reprinted with an Improved Index
Genealogical Publishing Co., Inc.
Baltimore, 1976

Reprinted for
Clearfield Company, Inc., by
Genealogical Publishing Co., Inc.
Baltimore, Maryland
1989, 1995, 1999, 2006

Library of Congress Catalogue Card Number 75-34969
International Standard Book Number: 0-8063-0704-8

Reprinted from a volume in
The North Carolina State Library
Raleigh, North Carolina

Copyright © 1976
Genealogical Publishing Co., Inc.
Baltimore, Maryland
All rights reserved

Made in the United States of America

FOREWORD

About the year 1927 the supervisors of Brunswick requested me to copy and index the marriage bonds of that county from 1752, when they began to appear in their loose papers, until our vital statistics commenced in 1852. From the beginning I listed them on cards, then entered them in a book. At first I thought of using these records in a forthcoming history of the county; however, after finding them sufficient for a separate volume I decided to let them stand on their own.

A few proofs of marriages prior to 1752 were located in estate settlements, as found in order books, and occasionally in will books or deeds. These I have from time to time entered in a special notebook, and so have included them here, giving sources. Those proofs of marriages other than bonds are listed as W. B., signifying Will Book; D. B. signifying Deed Book; and O. B. signifying Order Book.

When I undertook the work, the old bonds were torn and illegible and had to be examined under a strong light with a magnifying lens in order to piece out signatures and water marks.

I have used Eliz. for Elizabeth since it was written in several ways; also, Eliza is often mistaken as Elizabeth, which was also often written as Eliz[a] Securities on bonds were occasionally relatives of one or the other party to the marriage, otherwise the county clerk or some onlooker signed.

Augusta B. Fothergill

6 June 1856, Abernathy,Benjamin J.   to Anne E.Pritchett.

19 Dec.1814,   Buckner,   Nancy Lewis dau.of Ruel Lewis.

22 May 1764 by   Charles,   * * * Short dau.of William.W.B.III;537

14 Oct.1786,   "   Eliz.Davenport.Harbert Abernathy sec.

22 Nov.1802,   "   Nancy W.Croft

 5 Dec.1840,   "   Ann E.Johnson dau.of Wm.M.H.Johnson

 7 April 1809   Elisha   Nancy Read

11 Feb. 1795,   Frederick   Milly Davenport. Alexander Andrews sec.

22 Dec.1788,   Harbert   Susanna Harwell. Samuel Harwell sec.

10 Dec.1796,   Henry   Rebecca Firth,consent of Sarah Firth.

18 Feb.1828,   Hutchins   Sally Ann Stone

 9 Dec.1835,   Jackson   Susan Moore

22 March 1802   James   Francis M.Jennings dau.of Rebecca

 1 Feb.1809,   John   Nancy Kelly

25 April 1814,   "   Molly King

21 Aug. 1843,   " J.   Marietta A.Clayton

21 March 1820   Liles E.   Susan Vaughan

20 Nov.1827,   Mathew   Eliza Dixon dau.of John

 4 Jan.1816,   Rawleigh H.   Martha T.Avery

19 June 1843,   "   "   Susan Peterson

29 Dec.1849,   William C.   Rebecca Moore

15 Dec.1828,   Turner   Lucy W.Palmer dau.of W.Palmer

15 May 1818, Adams, Abner   Martha Ann Pettaway

27 Aug.1792,   David   Darcus Bass;Benj.Bass certified to age

10 Oct.1801,   Thomas   Lucy Orgain

26 Sept.1796,   Zadock   Eliz.Parish,William Parish sec.   1

2 Sept.1756,by, Adams, * * *   to   Eliz.Elzey dau.of John.(W.B.II;289)

10 Sept.1819,   Adkins,James M.   Mary J.Walker

18 July 1821,   " "   Sarah V.Collier

6 Oct.1810   Thomas   Creecy Birdsong dau.of Merrit B.

20 Apr.1810,   Alexander,John   Sally Thrower dau.Edward T.

9 Nov.1802,   William   Eliz.Lane dau.of Silvia Harris.

28 Nov.1785,   Allen,Howell   Mary Edwards, Harbert Edwards sec.

27 Aug.1792,   "   Rebecca Williams,Isaac Williams sec.

21 Sept.1815,   Jeremiah   Mary Ann Daniel

16 Jan.1845,   John   Rebecca F.Ferguson dau.Lockhart F.

30 Oct.1848,   " D.   Mary A.E.Bass

20 Sept.1819,   Redmon   Martha A.Bradley

28 July 1806,   Reuben   Elizabeth Lucy

14 Sept.1812,   "   Polly Burge

27 Dec.1792,   William   Lucy Brewer dau.of William,Morris Pearson sec.

7 Dec.1805,   "   Sally W.Tarpley

19 Dec.1805,   Wyatt   Nancy Tarver dau.of Andrew T.

3 May 1796,   Alley, * * *   Mynam Read dau.of James R.(W.B.VI; 66)

9 June 1834,   Allgood,Peterson   Tabitha J.C.Hudson dau.of George B.H.

13 Jan.1809,   Allmand,Edward   Mary Easter widow. William Pritchett sec.

24 July 1753,   Anderson,Claiborne of Chesterfield Co.   Betty Clack, James Clack sec.

5 March 1810,   Anderson, Caleb,   Frances L.James.

7 April 1779,   Churchill   Rebecca Hall dau.of Patrick.

29 Dec.1810,   Nathan   Eliz.Pritchett

15 Feb.1811,   Thomas   Martha J.Brock

22 Nov.1784,   Anderton,John   Clarisa Durham, Mordecai Howard sec.

22 Nov.1848, Anderton,Richard H.   to Matilda C.Turnbull

3 Nov.1796,   William   Macarina Ragland, Freeman Penticost sec.

8 Jan.1798, Andrews,Alexander   Martha Moore dau.of Thomas Moore.

29 Oct.1787,   "   David,   Eliz.(?) King. Howell Duggar sec.

28 May 1787,   "   John   Mary Edwards, John Edwards sec.

6 Apr.1802,by,   * * *   Lucretia Duggar dau of John Duggar.
                                      (W.B.VI;467)
14 Dec.1805,   "   Wilkins   Susanna Pegram

12 Jan.1788, Apelin,Thomas   Susanna McKenny, John McKenny sec.

21 Dec.1790, Archer,Amos   Fanny Harrison dau.of Thomas.Wm.Harrison
                                                                        sec.
23 Dec.1845,   Augustus C.   Rebecca Kelly

29 Dec.1827,   Edwin   Polly Hutchins

25 Oct.1808,   John   Jean Barrow

20 Dec.1819, Arnold,Joseph W.   Catherine Clayton

26 Dec.1825,   J.M.   Eliz.Laffoon dau.Simon and Milly L.

26 Dec.1786, Arrington,Richard   Catherine Carter.Freeman Malone sec.

22 Apr.1836,   William   Mary Short

29 Nov.1792,by,Aslin   * * *   Susanna McKinny dau.of John(W.B.V;575)

25 Nov.1794, Atkins,George   Mary Simms;Phil Claiborne sec.

3 Sept.1802,   "   Lucretia Taylor

22 June 1789,   William   Sarah Parham, James Parham sec.

8 Dec.1806,   "   Sarah Burge

13 June 1785,by,   * * *   Abigail Steed.(W.B.V;282)

26 Jan.1793,by,   * * *   Dousey Smith dau.of James.

15 Aug.1789,by, Atkinson * * *   Sarah Parham dau.of James.(W.B.V;415)

15 Feb.1823,   James W.   Charlotte E.Stith

25 Aug.1800,   John   Eliz.Lundie

4

18 Aug.1834, Atkinson, John P.	to Mary L.Harwell (Howell ?)	
27 Dec.1790,	Thomas	Eliz.Collier dau.of Charles.Wm.Atkinson sec.
26 Aug.1782,	William	Mary Hicks. Edward Tatum sec.
22 June 1789,	"	Sarah Parham dau.of Joseph.
22 June 1774,Avent,	Peter	Eliz.Sims. John Avent sec.
28 Nov.1825,	Thomas	Ann S.Powell dau.of Sarah S.Green.
19 Aug.1760,by,	* * *	Sarah Massie dau.of Joseph.
19 Aug.1760,by,	* * *	Amy Massie dau.of Joseph.(W.B.III;370.)
26 Jan.1829, Averett, William D.	Mary ANN J.Blick	
5 Dec.1843, Avery,Alexander	Blanche Abernathy dau.of John	
14 April 1834,	Archer,	Lucy Matthews dau.of Matthew
17 Mar.1800,	Barrington	Rebecca Mitchell
17 Oct.1836,	John E.	Patience Vaughan
26 Sept.1808,	Tilman	Temperence Edwards
13 May 1833,	"	Mary Abernathy
17 Feb.1858,	William V.	Eliz.Bass
29 July 1789,by,	* * *	Martha Morris (W.B.V;324)
14 Nov.1833, Baber, William D.	Julia H.Pollard	
16 Feb.1818, Bacon,Gillie M.	Eliz.M.Rhodes, William Palmer gdn.	
1 June 1813,	Thomas M.	Eliz.R.Gee
22 June 1840,Bagley,Edward G.	Martha E.Trotter	
20 Nov.1848,	George L.	Virginia J.Samford
24 June 1794,Bailey,Henry	Sarah Jackson, Henry Jackson sec.	
31 Mar.1794,	John	Jane Mitchell. William Mitchell sec.
28 Jan.1797,	"	Amy Dunman, Simon Lafoon sec.

22 Oct.1802, Bailey, Thomas S.	Hannah Jackson
5 April 1788, ***	Sarah Lanier dau.of Nicholas.(W.B.V;466)
28 Sept.1784,Baly, George	Eliz.Morris dau.of Henry.(O.B.XIV;12)
13 Feb.1809, Baird, John	Jean Read
25 March 1770,Baker, John	Patty Harris dau.of Henry Harris South.[n]
* " 1770, John	Patty Harris
27 Dec.1802,Balentine,Charles	Betty Brown
21 Dec.1836,Ball, William	Mary J.Simms
by Apr.1759,Ballard "	Eliz.Morris wid.of William.)O.B.VII;357
13 July 1813,Balthrop, "	Polly Blunt
23 Sept.1833,Bammer,David W.	Eliz. A.Nash
16 June 1817, John	Mary L.Collier
20 Sept.1807,Banks,William	Polly G.Jenkins
30 April 1830,Barham,John	Mary F.Jackson dau.of Mary Jackson
19 Dec.1836, William	Amaza A.Griffin
13 Feb.1806, Barner,Drury	Sally Taylor dau.of Luke and Eliz.T.
26 July 1797,by,Barker,* *	Milly Gunn dau.of William
27 Sept.1824, Barner,Drury J.	Martha H.Connelly dau.of William
17 Nov.1849, Ulyses	Penelope H.Harrison dau.of Willee
31 Dec.1778,by, ***	Patty Gresham dau.of John.(W.B.V;72)
29 Dec.1789,by, ***	Eliz.Harrison dau.of Benj.Sr.(W.B.V;345)
8Apr.1822,Barnes,Benjamin	Nancy Kelly dau.of William
28 Sept.1835, Edward H.	Mary A.Barnes
22 Jan.1827, Francis	Eliz.Bridgforth
22 Dec.1815, Henry,	Sally B.Rawlings
20 Mar.1788, James	Sally Browder dau.of Joseph and Suky

6 Jan.1802, Barnes, James   Nancy Hammond dau.of William

23 Sept.1835,   James M.   Susan Ann Tarpley

23 Dec.1848,   John J.   Eliza A.Daniel dau.of Peter

10 Dec.1776,by,   Stephen   * * * powers (W.B. IV;512)

23 Dec.1786,   "   Sarah Johnson, Allen Johnson sec.

9 July 1859,   Thomas H.   Mary Ann Walton
    s.of Henry

26 Oct.1835,   William   Eliza H.Connelly

21 Feb.1838,   "   R.   Frances J.Kennedy

12 May 1774,by,   * * ⸸   Hannah Andrews dau.of Joseph.

22 June 1793,Barnett, John   Nancy Nipper dau.of Jeams
    s.of John Sr.

25 Oct.1808, Barrow,Dennis   Ermine Daniel

10 Aug.1803,   John   Jincy Johnson dau.of John

26 Oct.1812,   "   Nancy Parker

1 Sept.1842,   "   Susan J.Dunkley

25 Dec.1821,   Lewis   Mary Rash

26 June 1839,   "   Mary Browder

21 Dec.1818   Thomas H.   Ann Morehead Dameron

12 Jan.1793,by,   * * *   Diana Daniel dau.of Joseph (W.B.V;550)

3 May 1796,   * * *   Nancy Read daughter of James(W.B.VI;66)

9 Apr.1830, Bartlett,Francis   Margaret Booth

31 July 1833,Barton, John   Susan C.Pryor

8 Jan.1817, Bass,   Allan   Sarah Adkins

4 Jan.1786,   Bertram   Rebecca Tatum, John Parish sec.

28 Apr.1803,   Edmund   Eliz.H.Ingram

25 Feb.1799,   Epharim   Patsey Lanier

25 Dec.1823,   Francis   Susan T.Williams

22 Feb.1797, Bass,	Frederick,Jr.	Polly Vaughan
27 Sept.1802,	Hartwell	Frances Mason
23 Dec.1778,	Henry	Eliz.Rivers dau.of William
3 March 1831,	James M.	Mary Ann Saunders
23 Jan.1827,	Jefferson	Mary Rideout dau.of Frances
21 Oct.1791,	John	Nancy Saunders. Thomas Saunders sec.
24 Oct.1791,	John H.	Rebecca Petillo, James Petillo sec.
28 Jan.1805,	Nathan	Martha Betty
21 Apr.1830,	Nathaniel	Mary Jane Jennings dau.of L.B.J.
14 Oct.1800,	Thomas	Sarah Adams.
28 March 1808,	"	Sally Fletcher
8 Nov.1827,	William S.	Hannah Vaughan
9 Oct.1773,	* * *	Mary Clark dau.of George
May 1752 , Bates, John		Tabitha Campbell wid.of Walter)O.B.IV; 175.)
2 Apr.1827, Batte,Richard C.		Sarah Ann Powell dau.of Eliz.
24 Jan.1822,	William	Eliz.Barker
1 Oct.1805,Baugh, Joel		Eliz,Haygood
17 June 1801,	Littleberry	Frances Wilkes
10 Dec.1820,	"	Martha Davis
5 Dec.1845	"	Rebecca Ann Hagood
22 Feb.1739,Bayles * * *		Jane Jackson dau.of John.
5 Sept.1790,Beasley, Barnet		Susanna Baugh dau.of Daniel
11 Jan.1836,	George W.	Mary Rollings
24 Aug.1812,	Peter J.	Martha E.Fletcher
19 Apr.1809,	" Dr.	Rebecca J.Fletcher
23 Nov.1842,	Richard R.	Martha E.Jones dau.of Robert K.

3 May 1796, Beck, * * *		Tabitha Read dau.of James
6 Mar.1738,by,Beddingfield,⌊Henry⌋		Martha Hicks dau.of Capt.Robert
19 Mar.1812, Belcher, John		Polly Hall
27 Apr.1840, Bell, Horace		Eliz.Buckner
19 Mar.1821, Bennett, Allen		Sally H.Archer
11 May 1808,	Benjamin	Susan Taylor
27 Nov.1848,	* M.	Susan A.E.Ragsdale
27 Apr.1801,	Maclin	Judith Bennett
1 Jan.1782,	Richard	Mary Crook dau.of James
9 July 1817,	s.of Benj. Richard F.	Mary Kirkland
22 Dec.1834,	Samuel	Frances W.B.Hill
5 Nov.1787,	William	Mary Edwards, Daniel Duggar sec.
9 Sept.1754,	* * *	Eliz.Proctor dau.of Robert (W.B.III; 263)
16 Jan.1773,by,	* * *	Martha Williams dau.of Williams(W.B.IV; 473)
5 June 1795,by,	* * *	Eliz.Sadler dau.of Thomas (W.B.III;46)
2 July 1767,by,Bentley,Samuel		* * * Spicer dau.of James (W.B.III;522)
25 Jan.1839, Bentley,David Meade		Sally Ann Field dau.of Richard W.
28 Apr.1787, Berry,John		Ann Ingram dau.of B.I.;John Lyell sec.
21 Dec.1811,	" J.	Mary W.Meredith
23 May 1844,	" J.	Martha E.Scoggin
1 Aug.1795,	William	Lucy Mathews dau.of Lucy, John Hampton sec.
9 July 1800,	"	Martha Collier
* * * 1818,Berthright,Peter,		Lucy Ogborne
22 Aug.1809, Berton,Thomas		Patsey Jarrett
24 Nov.1795, Beshars Jesse		Betsey Shell, William Shell sec.

27 Nov.1787, Bethshurs, Thomas		Eliz.Whitechurch,Peter Read sec.
25 July 1801,Betty, John		Lucy Petway
9 May 1797,	Thomas	Martha Preston dau.of Thomas,Has.P.sec.
31 Dec.1804,	"	Rebecca Finch
24 Dec.1787,	William	Mary Betty dau.of Thomas.Edward Thrower sec.
22 Jan.1798,	"	Ann Bass
7 Apr.1785, Biggs Joel		Nancy Elder dau.of Joseph,John Latimore sec.
15 June 1817,	Richard	Betsey Allen
15 Mar.1811,	Sterling	Nancy Howerton
19 May 1838,	William R.	Mourning Barrow.
12 Dec.1781,Bilbo James		Dorothy Clack, William Thornton sec.
7 Sept.1784,	Nicholas	Mary Baskerville, Hunt Baskerville sec.
11 Nov.1806,Billingsley,Elias		Lucy Powell
5 Sept.1801,Billups,Augustine		Sinah Vaughan
3 Jan.1822,	John	Susan J.Lanier dau.of Thomas
28 Nov.1823, Binford,Anderson A.		Sally Wall dau.of David
10 Aug.1797, Birchett,Edward		Polly Jackson, Benjamin Lewis guardian
5 July 1830,	Richard F.	Mary Ann Sharpe
4 Sept.1793,	Theodrick	Rebecca Collier dau.of Howell dec'd.
12 Oct.1770,by,	* * *	Eliz.Thweatt dau.of Jusdith (W.B.IV;165)
23 Mar.1795, Bird,	Battis	Susan Lawrence, Thomas Ingram sec.
25 Jan.1811, Birdsong,Henry		Polly House
10 Jan.1826,	James	Ann C.Lilly
10 Dec.1834,	" s.of John	Nancy James Harwell dau.of William Sr.
4 Nov.1826,	Nathaniel	Sally Short dau.of Griffin.
20 Apr.1789,	William	Judith Sealy,Merril Sealy sec.

10 Jan.1807,	Birdsong, William M.	Rebecca H.Bass
12 Feb.1774,by,	* * *	Mary Webb dau.of Eliz.
28 Aug.1827,	Bishop, Armistead	Ann Cheely
27 Nov.1752,by,	John	Rebecca Peebles dau.of Henry (D.B.V;385)
10 Jan.1793,	"	Eliz.Jones dau.of John of Crooked Run.
25 Sept.1821,	" N.	Eliz.Newsom
31 May 1793,	Joseph M.	Marticia Wynne dau.of Thomas.Wm.Bishop sec.
27 June 1798,by,	* * *	Polly Roberts dau.of William (W.B.VI; 511)
30 Mar.1792,	Blackwell,Robert	Jinny Jones dau.of Stephen.J.J.Jr.sec.
27 Aug.1810,	Blalock, Austin	Mansfield Moseley22
22 May 1786,	David	Kareh Vaughan, James Vaughan sec.
26 Dec.1796,	Richard	Tabitha Mize, Jeremiah Mize sec.
23 Feb.1779,	Blanks,Ingram	Patty Grigg, Mather Davis sec.
* June 1754,by,Blanks,Richard		Winifred House admx.of Lawrence House. O.B.V;221)
10 Mar.1799,by,	Blanch,Ezekiel	Sarah White sister of George.
10 Dec.1801,	"	Milly Cook dau.of Lencey Cook
20 Dec.1820,	George W.T.	Nancy B.Duggar
17 Nov.1849,	John S.	Ann E.Seward dau.of James
27 Dec.1834,	Bland, Dr.Theodrick	Mary B.Harrison dau.of L.W.H.
4 May 1842,	Blanks,Leodocius	Louisa Barnes dau.of John
9 Oct.1753,	Richard	Winifred House
15 Jan.1838,	William J.	Sarah P.Mitchell
23 Aug.1790,by,Blanton,	***	Patty Cleary dau.of Harwood.
4 Dec.1747,by,	Blaxton * * *	Sarah Cook dau.of Robert(O.B.II;145.)
3 Dec.1816,	Blick,Benjamin	Mary Ann S.Lanier
26 Nov.1785,	James	Sarah Baugh dau.of James deceased.

27 August 1787, Blick, James   to Catherine Lanier, William Lanier sec.

15 May 1828,   Blood, Oliver H.   Ellen W.Blake

10 Sept.1835,   Blunt, Walter F.   Argyra Harrison

14 Oct.1788,   William   Ann Gilliam dau.of John. Hinchia Gil-
                                                                     liam sec.
25 Nov.1816,   Bobbit, Lewis   Clementine Carter White dau.of John

26 May 1757,by, Boling * * *   Sarah Scoggin dau.of William

30 Nov.1811,   Bolling, Alexander   Elizabeth Tucker dau.of Wright
                 of Petersburg
24 June 1811,   Bolling, John   Jane Goode,ward of John C.Goode

 4 Oct.1790,   Robert   Katherine Stith dau.of Buckner.

 8 Sept.1807,   Samuel   Nancy W.Elliott, Philip Pryor sec.

13 Jan.1816,   Bonner,Jesse A.   Susan W.Atkinson

29 Oct.1810,   Booth,Benjamin   Sally Hicks dau.of Osaac.

24 June 1811,   Booth,Charles   Lucy Abernathy

23 Aug.1802,   Gilliam   Rebecca Hicks, Isaac Hicks sec.

 8 May 1822,   John   Jane A.Davis

26 Aug.1819,   Nathaniel   Nancy Kirk

27 Sept.1809   Robert C.   Eliz.B.Hicks

29 April 1835,   "   N.   Marietta E.Meade

24 July 1797,   Thomas   Martha Harrison, J.H.Harrison sec.

22 Sept.1803,   Bozeman,Thomas   Rebecca Aldridge

29 Apr.1834,   Bosseau,Edward L.   Evelina Barnes

 2 Jan.1826,   Boswell,Robert B.   Eliz.H.Shell

 3 Jan.1792,   William   Mary Wall dau.of George deceased

29 Aug.1800,   "   Susan Lane

 2 Jan.1810,   Bott, Edward Branch   Sally P.Parham dau.of William

 5 Jan.1823,   Luke   Rose Ann Percival

17 July 1800,	Bottom,	John	to	Tabitha Harrison
7 July 1823,	"	H.		Nancy Harrison
13 Aug.1798,	Bowen	Leonard		Priscilla Paup
12 Dec.1800,	Bowles,	Isaac		Timma Holloway
22 Dec.1792,		James Tomson		Milly Huff dau.of Daniel, William Huff sec.
26 Jan.1797,		John		Eliz.G.Barker dau.of Burrell
15 Dec.1802,	Bozeman,Edward			Susanna Quarles
12 Feb.1774,by,		* * *		Winifred Webb dau.of Elizabeth(W.B.IV; 208)
13 July 1835,	Bracey,	Leslie G.H.		Rebecca Mize
9 Dec.1833,		Paschal		Dorothy K.Turbeville dau.of Dorothy T.
1 April 1795,		Samuel		Tabitha Hicks dau.of Robert.
7 July 1823		Thomas H.		Mary W.Grigg dau.of W.Grigg
21 Dec.1790,by,		* * *		Mary Floyd dau.of Josiah(W.B.V; 396.)
28 Oct.1816,	Bradley,	John		Sarah Dailey
25 Nov.1778,by,		" dec'd		Mary Ledbetter dau.of Mary (W.B.V;58)
26 Aug.1833,	Bragg,David W.			Roberta C.Gilliam
24 June 1794,	Branch,Edward			Sally Goodrich dau.of Mary,Henry Bailey sec.
15 Feb.1797,		"		Martha Tilman
21 Dec.1840,		John E. s.of Miles B.		Mary S.Phipps dau.of John
16 Jan.1833,		Thomas C.		Eliza L.Bott
30 Nov.1815,	Branscomb,Benjamin			Tabitha Seward dau.of Joseph.
12 Nov.1823,		Thomas		Mary Ann Wyatt
9 Sept.1754,by,		* * *		Sarah Proctor dau.of Robert.(W.B.III; 263)
2 Oct.1793,		* * *		Amey Ingram dau.of Joseph.
28 April 1794,	Brann,	James		Nancy Porter dau.of John,Josh Porter sec.
10 Jan.1791,	Brantley,James			Rebecca Stainback. John Owen sec.

```
 7 July 1802, Brasington,Jesse       to   Martha Gladish

 8 Jan.1817,  Braswell,Jacob              Eliz.Seward daughter of Joseph

 3 Sept.1810,        Jesse               Winifred Nanny

23 Dec.1799,         John                Eliz.James

13 Feb.1847,         "  H.               Tabitha Nanny

28 Nov.1835,         Joseph P.           Nancy E.C.Jones dau.of William

16 Jan.1837,         Parham H.           Nancy G.Hill dau.of Hartwell

22 Dec.1834,         Pegram R.           Mary A.B.Atkins

25 Sept.1766,by,Breeding, * * *          Ann Read (W.B.IV;190)

21 Nov.1777,   Brent,Vincent             Margaret Brent, Robert Spencer sec.

27 Dec.1785,   Brewer,Bartlett           Biddy Cannon widow, Newit Brewer sec.

11 Apr.1747,by,     George               Abigail Wyche dau.of Francis(O.B.II;148)

26 Nov.1787,        John                 Mary Mitchell dau.of Lockhart

18 Dec.1805,        Kinshen              Patty Pearson

27 Nov.1821,        Lewis                Dorothy Brewer

27 August 1792,     Newit                Eliz.Nicholson, Isham Perkinson sec.

10 Jan.1822,        William              Sally Richardson

30 Dec.1816,        Willie               Tabitha Pearson

 4 Mar.1735,by,      * * *               Abigail Wyche dau.of Henry & Frances.
                                                            (Vol.1;256)
 1 Nov.1802,         * * *               Susanna Wheeler dau.of Benjamin.

10 Dec.1804, Bridge,  Thomas             Martha Bass

20 Jan.1792, Bridgforth,John             Mary Miller dau.of Jacob, Thomas Manson
                                                                          sec.
 4 May 1816,          Thomas             Lucy R.Collier

11 June 1759, Bridges,  Thomas           Dorothy Vines. Thomas Vines sec.

24 Feb.1772, Briggs,Frederick            Molly Goodrich,Edward Goodrich consent.

 9 July 1814,        Henry               Betsy H.Miskell
```

14

| 13 July 1774,by, Briggs,Howell, | to | * * * Quarles, dau.of John.(W.B.IV;481) |

13 July 1774,by, Briggs,Howell,   to   * * * Quarles, dau.of John.(W.B.IV;481)

23 Oct.1794,   William   Eliz.Reade dau.of William.(W.B.V;566)

9 Dec.1797,   * * *   Frances Eliz.Goodrich dau.of Mary

31 Dec.1794,   Brintle,Allen   Susanna Reese,Isham Reese consent

18 Oct.1832,   Robert   Rebecca Bass

10 Jan.1835,   Britt,   Benjamin J.   Hannah E.Powell

10 Nov.1797,   Isaac   Molly Monk Huff, James Huff sec.

24 Feb.1829,   "   Lucy B.Vaughan

20 Nov.1841,   "   Martha Ann Powell

3 Nov.1835,   Britton, Thomas W.   Temperance W.Jackson

23 July 1792,   Brock,Uriah   Martha Harrison, Benj.Lashley sec.

28 July 1794,   "   Silvia Huskey, William Huskey sec.

23 July 1781,   Brodnax, John   Martha Rivers dau.of Thomas.

* Dec.1785,   William   Sarah Jones

4 Dec.1747,by,Brook   * * *   Rebecca Cooke dau.of Robert (QBII;145)

9 Nov.1801,   Brooking,Edward B.   Rebecca Ann Jackson dau.of Ann.

8 Aug.1805,   Francis   Ann Smith dau.of Frederick

23 June 1817,   Browder, Caleb   Mary W.Scarbrough

27 Dec.1819,   David   Sally S.Thrower dau.of Christopher

24 Nov.1800,   John   Susanna Miller

8 March 1834,   "   Angelica F.Dameron dau.of Alexander

23 Dec.1811,   Joseph   Fanny Johnson dau.of William M.

29 Dec.1786,   Thompson   Tabitha Johnson, Joseph Browder sec.

9 May 1793,   Urias   Mary Quarles, William Quarles sec.

10 Apr.1817,   "   Sally Elmore, William Elmore sec.

19 Nov.1849,   William J.   Mary E.Scoggin

19 Dec.1778,	Brown,Rev.Aaron	to	Eliz.Harwell
25 Sept.1796,	Alexander		Jane Simmons ,Herbert Hill sec.
17 Nov.1778,	Arthur of N.C.		Mary Turner widow.
23 Nov.1795,	Davis		Martha Abernathy, John Abernathy sec.
* July 1791,	Jesse		Mason Hardaway
24 Feb.1800,	John		Eliz. Davis
28 Jan.1839,	" R.		Mary J.Parham dau.of Nicholas
3 Dec.1804,	Lewis		Fanny Duggar
25 Jan.1814,	" H.		Sally Avery
21 Dec.1830,	Paschal B.		Anana Daniel
24 Feb.1823,	Richard R.		Louisa H.Tatum
24 Oct.1803,	Stephen		Betsy L.Johnson
24 Oct.1803,	Thomas		Martha L.Trotter
16 Dec.1803,	" R.		Mary G.Baugh
12 Oct.1770,by,	Urvin		Mary Thweatt dau.of Judith.(W.B.IV;163)
3 Apr.1797,	William		Eliz.Lester, Thomas Lester sec.
8 Dec.1802,	"		Patsy Lucas dau.of Frederick
12 June 1736,	* * *		Ann Clark dau.of Samuel (D.& W.V.1;305)
28 Jan.1803,	Brumblo, * *		Amey Moseley dau.of William(W.B.VI;515)
22 Jan.1804,	Bryson,Robert		Ann E.Mason dau.of Margaret
7 May 1825,	Bruce,Robert H.		Julia A.G.Underhill dau.of John
28 Nov.1821,	Buckner, Charles D.		Mary M.H.Lynch dau.of Aiden
26 Nov.1804,	Buford,Abraham		Susan Ingram
1 June 1837,	"		Henrietta A.Hite
8 May 1833,	William P.		Lucy A.E.Rice
13 Feb.1849,	Buckley,James H.		Martha Ann Saunders dau.of Turner

20 May 1820, Buckley, John W.		to	Frances Kirkland
12 Dec.1849,	P.H.		Sally Kirkland
19 Feb.1845, Bugg	Jacob L.		Martha E.Seward dau.of James
9 Dec.1847,	" "		Lucy W.Hicks dau.of T.B.
29 Sept.1788	John		* * * Pennington sister of Sack(W.B.V; 554)
3 Feb.1798,	"		Sally Malone, George Malone sec.
29 Nov.1804,	"		Rebecca Seward
8 Jan.1742-3,Burch,	"		Eliz.Lanier, dau.of Sampson
30 May 1782,	"		Polly Firth dau.of Thomas
13 Feb.1809, Burdge, Beverley B.			Ann Jones
21 Nov.1810,	Drury		Eliz.C.Jones, George H.Jones sec.
20 Sept.1774,	Frederick		Frances Brown, Beverley Brown sec
11 Jan.1794	"		Betsey Kelley, Samuel Kelley sec.
25 Oct.1819,	"		Eliz.F.Smith daughter of Martha.
9 Dec.1813,	James		Eleanor H.Edwards
26 Feb.1818,	"		Nancy Birdsong
11 Jan.1820,	Wesley		Clara A.Dixon dau.of John.
15 Oct.1787	Wood		Eliz.Davis dau.of Hezekiah
24 Aug.1783,	* * *		Frances Brown (O.B.XIII; 224.)
7 Aug.1848,Burnett, John M.			Louisa Mason dau.of Nathaniel
8 Apr.1826,	Thomas M.		Lucretia Bishop dau.of Eliz.
16 Nov.1842,	William W.		Ann F.Burnett dau.of Mary A.H.Goodwyn
22 Dec.1818,Burrow, David			Ann E.Stainback dau.of Robinson
8 Feb.1795,	Gray		Nancy Parham, Batte Tatum sec.
11 Mar.1790,Burton,Hutchens			Ann Mitchell dau.of William

26 Dec.1828, Butler, Herod J.   to   Julia Ann Carpenter dau.of Winifred

16 Feb.1773,by,Butt * * *   Suckey Brown dau.of Richard (W.B.IV;148)

18 Nov.1847, Butts, Augustine C.   Anna M.Claiborne

14 Jan.1824,   Edmund L.   Eliz.B.Vaughan dau.of Susan

 8 Dec.1827,   " "   Eliz.Hawkins dau.of Smart

23 Sept.1776,   Thomas C.   Sarah Hunt, Robert Rivers sec.

11 Dec.1800, Burwell,Armistead   Mary Turnbull dau.of Robert

 9 Sept.1840, Bynum, Henry L.   Amanda M.Stith.

 8 Dec.1795, Byrne, James   Sarah S.Haskins, ward of John Haskins

 1 Dec.1818, Cabiness,John   Minerva Hicks

 8 Nov.1834,   William C.   Eliz.W.Phipps.

19 Jan.1841, Cain, James   Julia Ann Miller

13 Jan.1840,   John   Martha Valentine dau.of Isam

20 Apr.1784,   Mordecai   Sinah Saunders dau.of Edwin deceased

26 Nov.1785,   Peter   Eliz.Powell, Drury Dunn sec.

27 Dec.1785,   "   Scoty Mitchell, Thomas Mitchell sec.

11 May 1773,by,Calver, * *   Rebecca Wray dau.of John.(W.B.IV;204)

29 Nov.1792,by,Camp, * * *   Mary McKinney dau.of John (W.B.V;573)

 9 Dec.1780, Caudle, * * *   Frances Hardaway dau.of John.(W.B.V;87)

28 Jan.1803,by,Caudle,* * *   Eliz.Moseley dau.of William (W.B.VI;515)

18 March 1788,Callahan,David   Mary Dawson dau.of Samuel

29 Feb.1785, Callas, Henry   Sarah Morris, Robert Morris sec.

28 Nov.1816,   David   Sally Walpole

19 Jan.1829,   Henry   Ann Daniel

 5 Dec.1821,   Thomas   Jemima H.Walpole

20 May 1848, Callis,   Thomas H.   to   Sarah Elmore

24 Nov.1800, Camp,   Green   Polly Bsandus

10 Jan.1799,   Jesse   Sally Wallace

26 Aug.1793,   John   Patsy Justys, George Johnson sec.

19 Dec.1829,   Peter G.   Mary E.Rainey

22 Oct.1821,   William P.   Lucy C.Foster

 1 June 1831,Campbell, Lewis   Susan Julia Jones

12 June 1793,   Parsons   Susanna Ezell, Archibald Ezell sec.

14 Feb.1752,   Robert   Mary Neal, Lewis Parham sec.

28 Mar.1822,   "   Sally B.Ivie

20 March 1802,Cardwell,George   Elizabeth Hicks dau.of John

16 Mar.1790, Cargill, John A.   Rachel Lester dau.of Eliz.,Whited Lester
                                                                    sec.
23 Nov.1801, Carpenter,Isaac   Winifred Brewer

24 Mar.1789,   John   Rachel Brewer, James Brewer sec.

25 Mar.1744,   "   S.   Jane Richardson

20 Nov.1806,   Marshall   Jensey Saunders dau.of John

25 Jan.1847,   "   Rebecca Brewer

20 Dec.1803,   Richard   Retta Rhea

28 Dec.1795,   William   Polly Manning, William Manning sec.

17 Dec.1798,   Willis   Tempy Wray, Brittain Wray sec.

 9 Dec.1835, Carrell, Jordan W.   Ann Barner

 3 May 1796,by,   * * *   Rebecca Read dau.of James. (W.B.VI;66)

 9 Dec.1835, Carroll, William G.   Nancy Jett

 8 Mar.1790, Carrington,Patrick   Fanny Johnson, William Johnson sec.

 1 May 1822,   Thomas   Nancy Singleton

28 Dec.1832,   "   Eliz.Singleton

29 May 1813, Carroll, Solomon S. to   Frances S.Douglass

29 May 1813,   Thomas   Rebecca Shell

3 Jan.1803, Cates,   Richard   Nancy Potts

23 Jan.1754, Carter,   John   Rebecca Stuart,   James Jones sec.

30 Mar.1758,   Joseph   Mary Robertson,   Arch.^{d} Wager sec.⌊Clerk⌉

23 Sept.1741,by,Cator,   * * *   Jane Cook dau.of Henry(D.B.II;97)

17 July 1786,by,   "   * * *   Eliz.Manning dau.of John.(W.B.V;283.)

13 June 1814,Cattles,John   Martha Ann Moore dau.of Benjamin

25 Jan.1779, Caudle, William   Frances Hardaway

6 Nov.1784,   William   Martha Hall widow of John.

30 Jan.1778, Celey,   Merrit   Obedience King,   Charles King sec.

1 Jan.1746,   Chamberlayne,Charles   Hannah Turner dau.of Thomas(O.B.III;124)

3 Feb.1824,   Chambers,Edward R.   Lucy G.Tucker dau.of John of Prestwood.

18 Jan.1797,Chambliss,James   Rebecca Atkinson

24 Dec.1777,   Joel   Mary Bailey dau.of Robert,Henry Chamblis sec.

3 Jan.1799,   John   Jane Rideout dau.of William.

20 Dec.1824,   Thomas A.   Evelina Smith dau.of Frederick

21 Dec.1767,   * * *   Lucy Williams dau.of Jane (W.B.IV;65.)

6 Dec.1824,Chapman,   John   Mary Hagood,dau.of Randolph

24 Jan.1758,   William   Tabitha Wyche wid. Richard Kello sec.

5 Oct.1759,   "   Ezabel Kemp, Edward Robinson sec.

11 Mar.1783,   "   Martha Williamson dau.of Charles.

3 Mar.1788,   * * *   Rebecca Goodrich dau.of Briggs.(W.B.V; 278)

8 Mar.1763,Chappell   * * *   Nancy Harrison,dau.of Joseph.(W.B.IV; 347)

31 Dec.1806,Charles, John W.   Nancy Maclin, Frederick Maclin sec.

10 Feb.1834,Cheatham,Robinson B.   Eliza G.Allen

15 Dec.1798, Cheatham, Wyatt   to Poll, Barker,dau.of Burrell

13 Nov.1792, Chealy,   * * *   Winifred Lenoir dau.of Robert (W.B.V;510)

24 Apr.1797, Cheely,John   Fanny Short dau.of John

22 Dec.1823,   "   Mary French Judd

10 Sept.1840,   " H.   Louisa S.Johnson dau.of Thomas

22 Dec.1828   Joseph   Diana J.Chambliss

12 Nov.1827,   Thomas W.   Louisa A.Smith

7 Jan.1846,   William W.   Mary F.Cheely dau.of John

20 Sept.1766,Chick,   * * *   Ann Cocke dau.of Brazure.(W.B.IV;32)

28 Jan.1798, Christian,Edward   Patsey Morris, Sherod Morris sec.

12 Nov.1800,   John   Sally Sills

27 Mar.1800,   * * *   Tabitha House dau.of Isham (W.B.VI;293)

27 Dec.1830, Childers,Benjamin   Cadijah Thomas

21 Dec.1792, Chiles,   John   Loise Browder, Joseph Browder sec.

31 May 1802, Crichton, James   Sally Winfield

14 Sept.1786,Clack,Richard   Ann Hardaway, James Stainback sec.

3 June 1794,   "   Amey Maclin, Frederick Maclin sec.

6 Oct.1847,   Robert K.   Eliz.Percival

16 Oct.1757,   William   Betty Twitty, Thomas Twitty sec.

27 Sept.1814,   " E.   Rebecca James

17 May 1817, Claiborne, Dr.Deveroux J.Dr.Harriet Edmunds dau,of Thomas.

2 May 1831,   " J.   Maria Lewis orphan Nicholas decd.

20 Apr.1836,   " "   Martha Lewis,

25 June 1849,   " J.Sr.   Sally A.Taylor

14 Sept.1798,   John   Sally Clayton, Phil Claiborne sec.

23 Sept.1802,   "   Nancy Jones

8 Jan.1832, Claiborne,	John C.	to	Caroline Worthington
26 May 1817,	Phil		Eliz.Wilkes
30 May 1818,	Philip		Martha J.Claiborne dau.of Phil
25 Nov.1805,	Thomas Jr.		Hannah Hicks
27 Sept.1790,Clanton,	George		Anney Wills, John Wills sec.
31 Jan.1783, Clark,	Elisha,		Mary Hardaway,widow. Lewis Brown Jr.sec.
5 Nov.1806,	John		Eliza Murrell
30 Nov.1799,Clarke,	Edwin		Polly Thompson dau.of Christopher
16 Nov.1836,	E.F.		Mary W.Harrison
25 Nov.1819,	George W.		Jane Shelton
4 Dec.1825,	Henry		Rebecca Ann Delbridge dau.of Thomas
11 Sept.1826,	James		Nancy B.Taylor dau.of Nancy
12 Nov.1821,	Joshua		Anny Neale
* * 1821,	Thomas		Wilmouth Strange
25 April 1826,	Thomas W.		Mary A.H.Coleman
12 Mar.1827,	William E.		Polly Taylor
6 June 1826,	" H.		Susan G.Wilson
28 Nov.1786, Clary,	Benjamin		Winifred Kelly, David Kelly sec.
24 Dec.1844,	George		Louisa Kelly dau.of Martha.
30 July 1831,	Henry		Sarah R.Eldridge
18 Dec.1820,	Herod		Martha Wesson
2 Jan.1788,	John		Sarah Moseley, William Moseley sec.
10 Dec.1807,	"		Middy Edmunds
27 Dec.1786,	Thomas		Sarah Moseley, Peter Read sec.
19 Jan.1779, Clay,	John		Patty Ingram dau.of John. Moses Ingram sec.
7 Aug.1823,	Joseph W.		Rebecca E.H.Vaughan

31 Oct.1842, Claybrook, Chastain   to   Katherine Malone

28 Dec.1828, Clayton,   Edward   Eliza M.Davis

26 Nov.1776,   John   Temperence Hill,G.Hill's consent.

27 Dec.1790,   *   Sarah Harris, Charles Harris sec.

 8 May 1838,   "   Clara Short

13 Dec.1800,   William   Mary Williams dau.of Miles

 6 Dec.1787,   * * *   Susanna Short dau.of William.(W.B.V;203)

17 Oct.1821, Cleaton,   John   Penelope Preston, Jones Preston sec.

28 Sept.1788,   Thomas   Anne Barrow, Thomas Washington sec.

24 Aug.1835,   William B.   Eliza J.Davis.

 5 Feb.1840, Clemens,   Reuben W.   Sarah Adams orphan aged 23 years.

 2 Dec.1772, Clements   Thomas   Amey Maclin dau.of James.

15 Feb.1777, Clifton   * * *   Dorcas Turner.(W.B.IV;506)

17 Feb.1790, Clough,   Richard   Jane Thornton, Sterling C.Thornton sec.

17 Dec.1787, Cocke,   Abraham   to Anne Hardy dau.of Richard. B.White-
                                                                      head sec

 7 July 1821,   John H.   Anne H.Pritchett

 * May 1769,   Peter   Mary Whitehead dau.of Richard.

 * Mar.1775,   Thomas   Eliz.Willis. Richard Peete sec.

24 Mar.1772,   William   Mary Maclin dau.of William.

* * *   1750s   William   Rebecca Edwards, Nathaniel Edwards sec.

21 Oct.1829,   William A.   Nancy Patillo dau.of Martha

 1 Nov.1806, Coe,   Jesse   Selah D.Gilliam

21 Apr.1830, Cokeley   John   Susan J.Nolly

11 July 1819,Cole,   George,   Martha Grimes dau.of Frances Bass.

15 Jan.1817,   Hamlin   Martha Morriss

 9 Sept.   "   Angelica Bishop

23 Nov.1836, Cole, James   to   Frances Vaughan

13 Feb.1745,   John J.   Jane Daniel

24 Dec.1838,   " R.   Martha J.Webb

12 Dec.1820,   Sterling   Rebecca Ferguson dau.of Horatio

22 Feb.1817,   Thomas   Eliz.Moore

 1 Dec.1821,   William   Eliz.Barrow dau.of John.

 7 Feb.1842, Coleman, Henry W.   Maria L.Cheely

29 Dec.1814,   John   Eliz.H.Walker

25 Sept.1836,   " B.   Susan W.Pritchett

10 Apr.1812,   Nathaniel   Eliz.Cheely, Edward Randolph sec.

18 Oct.1794,   Richard   Mary Harper dau.of Nathaniel(W.B.V;557)

23 Dec.1808,   "   Dorothy Atkinson

 8 Sept.1830,   Wiley G.   Eliz.Rawlings

29 Jan.1810,   Williamson   Martha Burge

20 Sept.1766,   * * *   Susanna Cocke dau.of Brazure.(W.B.IV;32)

 3 July 1840, Coley, * * *   Eliz.Cooke.

16 Dec.1799, Collier,Benjamin   Middleton Brewer dau.of Jesse

 5 Sept.1787,   Edmund   Ann Washington, Joseph Browder sec.

 6 Jan.1796,   "   Judith Hicks dau.of John.

10 Dec.1779,   Emanuel   Susannah Morris dau.of Thomas

23 Nov.1807,   Henry   Milly Britt, Edmund Collier sec.

 3 Oct.1792,   Ingram   Susanna Browder, Edmund Collier sec.

22 Sept.1777,   (Lewis)   Eliz.Hagood dau.of John.

30 Oct.1797,   Miles   Nancy Gee, Joshua Gee sec.

 1 Sug.1769,   Moses   Nancy Blank, John House sec.

26 Nov.1769,   Myhill   Tabitha Harrison dau.of Benjamin.

```
17 Sept.1802,  Collier,  Nathaniel  to   Sally Williamson

19 Jan.1791,             Smith            Patsy Atkinson dau.of William

22 Nov.1773,             William          Patty Thweatt dau.of Miles.

20 Dec.1781,             "                Mary Gee dau.of William, John Gee sec

20 May 1802,             "  S.            Sally Watson

18 Feb.1843,             "  T.            Jane Ferguson dau.of Lockett

24 May 1770,             * * *            Mary Peebles dau.of John.(W.B.IV;113)

 5 Feb.1833,  Collins    Luke            Midia Pearson

29 July 1789,            * * *            Sarah Morris dau.of Thomas(W.B.V;324)

29 July 1789,            * * *            Susanna Morris dau.of Nich.(W.B.V;324)

30 Oct.1807,  Connell,   Robert          Anna Smith dau.of Ely & Mary.

22 Dec.1842,             Wesley          Susanna A.Mathews

31 Dec.1799,  Connelly,  Daniel          Eliz.King dau.of Charles

11 Dec.1828,             Edward          Harriet W.Ogburn dau.of John.

17 Dec.1832,             Ira             Mary Jane Rebecca Jennings dau.of Susan

22 May 1803,             Lewis           Lucy Alley

 3 Feb.1836,             Robert          Mary ANN P.Bottow.

17 Mar.1790,             William         Sally Fort dau.of Martha

 6 Dec.1841,             "  M.           Sarah J.Barrow

16 Dec.1828, Converse,   Amasa           Flavia Booth

24 Sept.1759,Cook,       John s.of Henry Betty Brown, John Peterson sec.

12 June 1736,            * * *            Mary Clark dau.of Samuel.(Vol.1;305.0

28 Dec.1789,             * * *            Rita Harrison dau.of Benjamin Sr.(W.B.V;
                                                                         345)
- -Nov.1790, Cooper,     Edward          Patsy Jackson, Wm.E.Brodnax sec.

20 Dec.1820,             Edmund          Susan Abernathy

16 Aug.1796, Coocey,     Charles         Sarah King dau.of Nathaniel
```

3 Jan.1793,	Cooksey,	Hezekiah	to	Ann Rivers dau.of Ann Peebles
11 May 1766,	Copeland,	* * *		Sarah Lindsay dau.of William(W.B.III;512
20 Feb.1794,	Coppage,	Isaac		Sarah Jackson, Moses Lunsford sec.
22 Dec.1800,	Cordle,	Charles		Tabitha Harrison
16 Dec.1823,	"	John		Martha J.Walton
22 Sept.1845,		"		Polly Smith
26 Feb.1814,		William		Martha Greenhill
26 Mar.1793,	Cotten,	Thomas		Sarah Hall over 21 yrs.,Geo.Johnson sec.
14 Oct.1756,	Courtney,Dr.Clack			Prudence Clarke dau.of George.
* * * 1817,	Cox,	Fleming,		Jincey Morriss dau.of Sherod.
19 Mar.1847,	Crawley,Robert H.			Martha A.Pritchett dau.of R.F.
May Ct.1756,	Craft,	Thomas		Eliz.Burch widow of John.(O.B.VI;21)
23 Dec.1782,		Washington		Polly Berry dau.of George deceased.
22 Jan.1783,		"		Molly Berry dau.of George deceased(O.B. XIII;100)
22 Oct.1792,		"		Mary Tilman, William Parham sec.
24 Nov.1834,	Crechton,Thomas W.			Ann E.Rawlings
6 Nov.1848,	Crenshaw,Ira J.			Martha Jane Gregg
11 July 1818,Crittenden,William				Susan Bridgforth
15 Dec.1811,	Crook,	David		Rebecca Adkins
26 May 1800,		Giles		Sarah W.Kelley dau.of Samuel
23 Dec.1793,		James		Fanny Robinson, Xpher Robinson sec.
24 May 1790,		John		Rebecca Nash dau.of John; Josh.Lucy sec.
21 Jan.1783,		Joseph		Eliz.Berry dau.of George deceased
4 Sept.1806,		"		Eliz.G.Collier
26 Jan.1808,		Robert		Sally McKenny dau.of James
3 Feb.1813,		Thomas		Eleanor House

23 July 1770,	Cross,	Richard	to Ann Maclin dau.of William, Wm.Clack sec.
26 Feb.1803,	Crow	John	Martha Briggs
25 Nov.1805,	Crowder,	Bartho-lew	Jane C.Thompson
21 May 1763,		James	Sarah Doley dau.of William
8 Nov.1804,		Miles	Eliz.B.Thompson
25 Dec.1849,		Nathiel R.	Martha P.Westmoreland
19 Sept.1842,		Sterling	Sarah W.Stanley
9 Dec.1795,		Thomas	Mary Jordan, John Jordan sec.
15 Jan.1793 ?,		William	Phebe Elder, Thomas Grubbs sec.
5 April 1788,		* * *	Mary Lanier dau.of Nicholas(W.B.V;466)
1 Feb.1791,	Cullum	William	Dorcas Stegall, Samuel Stegall sec.
12 Oct.1795,	Curd,	Richard	Nancy Harrison, Thomas Harrison sec.
25 Jan.1779,	Curdle,	William	Frances Hardaway, John Hardaway sec.
18 Oct.1799,	Dailey,	Andrew	Huldy Collins
24 April 1797,		Arthur	Jane Parrish, Thomas Parrish sec.
7 Aug.1788,		Denice	Mildred Smith, Theophilus Harrison sec.
7 Dec.1818,		John	Ann C.Thrower dau.of Mary
2 Mar.1829,	Daly	Arthur	Rebecca Saunders
9 Sept.1788,	Dameron,	Alexander	Becky Lightfoot, Alexander Dameron s
25 Dec.1821,		Bartho.	Nancy Read (Reid)
5 Dec.1836,		William H.	Julia Mangum
11 Dec.1787,	Dance,	Thomas	Sarah Fisher,dau.of James deceased
9 Sept.1779,	Dancey,	Francis	Sarah Turner wid.,James Mason sec.
20 Nov.1825,	Dandridge,	William F.	Susan C.Stith
15 Dec.1797,	Daniel,	George,	Armon Brown dau.of William
23 July 1838,		Gilliam	Eliz.A.Vaughan

23 Dec.1806, Daniel, Hezekiah   to   Nancy Lewis Tarpley

13 Apr.1840,   "   Mary Hammons

15 Jan.1798,   Joseph   Sally Cordle

25 Sept.1844,   "   Sarah J.Pritchett

4 Dec.1833,   Mathew   Eliz.D.Clarke

21 Oct.1821,   Math,   Lucy Day

26 Feb.1816,   Peter   Eliz.Parker

13 Dec.1838,   Pryor   Susan Elmore dau.of James

3 Jan.1826,   Richard   Ermond Pritchett

7 Jan.1791,   Robert   Martha Hawks 21, Randolph Stegall sec.

31 Jan.1814,   Thomas   Milly Barrow.

10 Dec.1847,   "   Amelia F.Johnson dau.of Nancy

23 Jan.1843,   Wesley   Susan M.Robins dau.of Solomon

15 Feb.1825,   William   Sally B.Foster dau.of John H.

31 Jan.1807,   "   R.   Polly Barrow

16 Feb.1773,   * * *   Sarah Brown dau.of Richard (W.B.IV;148)

11 Nov.1801, Davis,   Allen W.   Priscilla Gee

19 May 1802,   Edward   Eliz.Boswell

11 Nov.1837,   "   Frances A.Hicks

18 May 1844,   "   H.   S.A.Orgain

13 Feb.1849,   Henry R.   Ann E.Lewis

3 Mar.1795,   Hezekiah   Mary Pritchett dau.of William

4 Oct.1803,   Holland,   Polly Bruce dau.of James

16 Jan.1801,   James   Lucy Walker

22 Dec.1795,   John   Pheobe Floyd dau.of Charles(W.B.VI;82)

4 Feb.1796,   "   Frances Collier, Charles Collier sec.

```
 8 Dèc.1798, Davis,  John            to  Jane Abernathy dau.of John Sr.

28 Aug.1798,          "                Eliz.Howerton

30 Dec.1846,          "                Lucy Cammell

29 Nov.1848,          " H.             Elvira Nanny dau.of Isaac

23 Oct.1843,          " R.H.W. s.of Ro.Ann B.Pool dau.of John W.P.Pool

26 Mar.1770,         Joshua            Ann Smith, Cuthbert Smith sec.

 9 June 1795,        Lewis             Bridgett Gee dau.of William,(W.B.VI;73)

22 Mar.1773,         Mathew            Tabitha Tuell, Lawrence House sec.

25 Oct.1784,         Randolph          Hannah Marriott dau.of Thomas,(W.B.V;
                                                                    316)
27 Jan.1803,         Slayton           Polly Ingram

20 Dec.1802,         Sterling          Rebecca Caudle

29 Aug.1769,         William           Agness Lanier dau.of Sampson

23 Nov.1772,          "                Martha * * *            O.B.XII;156)

 9 Jan.1815,          "                Ann Pennington

 4 Apr.1818,          "                Eliz.Jones

16 May 1835,          " E.             Ann E.Drummond

31 Dec.1849,          " L.             Julia B.Pritchett dau.of Edmund W.

24 Jan.1816,         Willis S.         Sarah M.Thompson dau.of Robert

25 Feb. 1775,         * * *            Mary Rosser dau.of John(W.B.IV;471)

 7 Aug.1780,          * * *            Tabitha Rose dau.of John

16 Jan.1756, Dawson,  Samuel of Amelia Martha Jones dau.of Thomas of Brun.

13 Jan.1794, Day,    Lewis             Polly Lanier 21, Epharium Jackson sec.

29 Mar.1798,         Jesse             Eliz.Hearn, John Hearn sec.

21 Feb.1833,         John W.           Frances Daniel

24 Nov.1800 Dean,    Robert            Patty Clements

11 Nov.1826,          " s.of Robert    Eliza Williams
```

25 Oct.1843, Dean,	Robert Sr.	to	Mary Holloway
1 Feb.1830, Deane,	Anderson		Lucy Lanier dau.of David
25 Apr.1759, Dearden,	George		Martha Burch, Will Thornton sec
26 Oct.1789, Delayney	John		Sarah Ingram, John Atkins sec.
22 May 1802, Delbridge, Benjamin			Sally Jackson dau.of Epharium & Sally.
3 May 1817,	"		Lucy Wallon
28 May 1804,	Thomas		Sally Woolsey
3 Feb.1840,	" D.		Lucy P.Walton
29 Sept.1818,	Turner		Susan R.Allen
15 Dec.1811,	Warren		Betsey Phillips dau.of Thomas
11 May 1755, Deloney,	Henry of Lun.		Rebecca Walker, John Maclin sec.
8 Mar.1825, Dener,	John J.		Tabitha H.Batte dau,of William.
25 Oct.1796, Denton,	Benjamin		Mary Manning, Caleb Manning sec.
4 April 1744, "	Edward		Isabel Sisson dau.of Thomas(D.B.II;472)
4 " 1744	Thomas		Mary Sisson (D.B.II;468)
14 Apr.1802, Derby,	John		Lucy Porter
20 June 1840,Dillon,	Alex.S.,Dr.		Mary Claiborne dau.of D.J.Sr.
* May 1818, Dickerson,	James		Rebecca B.Carrington
27 Mar.1815, Dicks,	William		Fanny Scarborough
21 May 1763, Dillard,	John		Mary Doby dau.of William(W.B.IV;109)
28 Jan.1799, Dixon,	John		Rebecca Abernathy
7 Jan.1796, Dismang,	David		Eliz.Tilly, John Tilly sec.
23 Aug.1802, Bobbins,	Bowler		Ann Hearn
24 Sept.1788,	* * *		Patty Birchett dau.of Jane(W.B.V;341)
24 June 1818,Doyal,	Willey		Sally Mitchell dau.of Banister
* * Mar.1819,Doyle, Rev.John			Nancy W.Tarpley dau.of John & Sally

24 Apr.1826, Doyle,   John,   to   Catherine Barrow

14 Apr.1848,   John W.   Sarah E.Jolly

12 Aug.1802, Drake   Thomas   Caty Vaughan

 5 March 1777,Dromgoole,Edward   Rebecca Walton dau.of John

12 Dec.1828,   John E.   Lucy K.Blanch

25 Dec.1815, Drummond, Allen B.   Mary B.Wilkes

11 Jan.1823,   Grieve   Eliz. Starke

10 Dec.1791,   John   Katherine Love, Allen Love sec.

13 Aug.1845,   " B.   Harriet R.Northington dau.of John W.S.

28 Jan.1806, Drumright,James W.   Eliz.Saunders dau.of Mary

28 Jan.1839,   William   Mildred Nance

 8 Dec.1825, Duane,   Timothy,   Mary A.House

21 Dec.1832, Duggar, Ezra   Lucy A.L.Pritchett dau.of John

 4 Sept.1787,   German   Eliz.Price dau.of Joseph

 7 Feb.1792,   Henry Jr.   Armon Dugger dau.of Lurany Price

23 Aug.1820,   "   Anneliza Clayton

21 Dec.1795,   Howell   Polly B.Firth, William Firth sec.

12 Sept.1787,   James   Nancy Brown dau.of Lewis.

 4 Sept.1791,   "   Nancy Edwards, Jesse Edwards sec.

22 Dec.1814,   "   Eliz.W.Lucas

24 Jan.1791,   Jarman   Mary Rainey, Daniel Duggar sec.

22 Dec.1821,   John   Sally E.Parish

17 Dec.1840,   " C.   Cinthia J.Walker dau.of Permela

14 Dec.1814,   Joseph   Martha Peebles dau.of Jesse

22 Apr.1799,   Richmond   Eliz.Crowder

 7 Apr.1789,   Sterling   Sally Dugger, John Dugger sec.

27 Nov.1828, Duggar, Sterling   to Frances Parish

 5 June 1795,   * * *   Fanny Sadler dau.of Thomas (W.B.VI;46)

11 Nov.1748 Duke,   John   Rejoice Davis dau.of John.(W.B.III;40)

 3 June 1737,   William   Eliz.Bartholomew wid.of John.(O.B.1;171)

15 Aug.1789,   * * *   Mary Parham dau.of James.(W.B.V;415.)

 6 Apr.1802,   * * *   Mary Duggar dau.of John.

 5 Sept.1797,Dunkin, * * *   Anna Preston dau.of Thomas.

15 April 1805,Dunkley,Robert   Nancy Barrow dau.of William & Nancy

 7 Aug.1817,   Zarel,   Lucy Biggs dau.of Richard

 3 Apr.1843, Dunn, John H.   Susan M.J.Harris

23 Mar.1789,   Thomas   Eliz.Collier, Isaac Hicks sec.

 6 Feb.1759, Dupree, James   Mary Adams

15 Feb.1780,   "   Mary Adams dau.of Isaac

29 Nov.1830, Dupriese,Justinian   Minerva W.Jones dau.of Mary Jones

 4 Feb.1833, Dupuy, Joel W.   Paulend P.Eldridge

22 Oct.1788, Dunnington,Walter   Nancy Judd, John Judd sec.

 9 Mar.1822, Dunnivant, Haley   Julia Vaughan

11 June 1787,   William of Pr.Ed.Eliz.Samford dau.of Milly.

 2 June 1838, Dunwell, George C.   Judith S.Jackson dau.of Mary

24 Oct.1831, Eanes,   Edward D.   Mary H.Winn

26 May 1835,   Richard O.   Martha A?Winn dau.of Martha R.

22 June1778, Early,   Jaconus   Sally Wall, Daniel Call sec.

17 Sept.1788, Easter, John   Mary Walker widow pf David,Jos Lyell sec.

 8 Dec.1781, Eaton , Tho,as   Ann Stith dau.of Buckner,Buckner Stith
                                    Jr.sec.

 6 Nov.1815, Edmundson,Samuel,   Nancy Jones,dau.of Robert.

16 Nov.1792,   Upton,   Martha Hightower ,

27 Feb.1815, Edmunds, Benjamin,   to Martha Haskins dau.of John

22 Apr.1844,   Edwin H.   Sarah E.Lattimore

 9 Jan.1828,   Nicholas S.   Martha A.Harrison

31 Dec.1810,   Richard   Helen Wray Stuart

28 April 1794,   Samuel   Betsey Saunders dau.of Thomas

28 Nov.1774,   Sterling   Ermine Simmons, John Flood Edmunds sec.

21 Dec.1821,   "   H.   Martha Kirkland

25 Nov.1771,   Thomas   Sarah Eldridge, John Ballard Jr.Sec

22 Sept.1828,   "   D.   Susan J.H.Fisher

25 Nov.1793,   Wyatt   Rebecca Beck, James Huff sec.

15 Feb.1790,   * * *   Rebecca Harmon dau.of George.(W.B.VI;96)

20 Nov.1805, Edwards,Benjamin   Martha Haskins dau.of Elizabeth

25 Nov.1810   "   Eliz. Nanny

28 Apr.1828,   "   T.   Matilda R.Harris

25 Mar.1793,   Burwell   Lucy Stewart, Richardson Brown sec.

18 Jan.1786,   David   Lucy Weathers, Lewis Browb sec.

15 May 1786,   Gray,   Eliz.Ingram wid.of Moses, Wash.^{n} Craft
                                                                          sec.
19 Dec.1792,   Herbert   Charlotte Williams dau.of Lawrence

12 Mar.1798,   "   Sarah Stainback, Thomas Edwards sec.

11 May 1756,   Hugh   Sarah Daniel dau.of Peter

28 Mar.1798,   Jesse   Betsey Williams, David Williams sec.

29 June 1785,   John   Eliz.Rainey dau.of William

 7 Nov.1793,   "   * * * Simmons dau.of Susanna(W.B.V;521)

19 Aug.1820,   "   Eliza Goodwyn

14 Mar.1786,   Lewis   Rachel Wright, George Wright sec.

 2 Feb.1814,   Littleberry   Nancy Seward dau.of Joseph.

10 Oct.1787,	Edwards,	Nathaniel	to Mary Tatum dau.of Paul dec'd
25 Aug.1818,		Peter	Martha Stainback
18 Nov.1807,		Sampson	Polly B.Marks.
28 Nov.1778,		Shirley	Ermine Simmons, John Flood Edmunds sec.
25 Oct.1798,		Thomas	Eliz.Hancock
22 Sept.1806,		"	Sally Ingram
21 Ja.1807,		"	Nancy Mathews
5 Jan.1766,		William	Susanna Simmons dau.of Henry
L Dec.1771,		"	Susanna Maclin, John Maclin Jr. sec.
25 Sept.1815,		"	Sarah Nanny dau.of Drury
51 Mar.1787,		* * *	Bromley Rawlings dau.of William(W.B.V; 202)
6 Oct.1793,		* * *	Mary Myrick
22 Aug.1785,	Elder,	David	Polly Read dau.of William,Joel Biggs sec.
23 Jan.1797,		"	Polly Philips dau.of Thomas
22 Dec.1800,		Jonathan	Patsey Seward, Joseph Seward sec.
12 Mar.1806		Peter	Tabitha Kirkland
1 June 1785,	Eldridge,	Aristotle	Ann Lanier dau.of Buckner.Thos.Saunders sec.
8 Sept.1817,		George G.	* * * Adams
7 Dec.1827,		*** *	Mary Ann R.Smith dau.of Sally
27 May 1782,		Howell	Martha Fisher dau.of James, Thos.Edmunds sec.
25 Nov.1773,		Rolf	Susanna Walker dau.of George.
14 April 1829,		Thomas	Nancy Rawlings
19 Dec.1820,		William H.	Eliz.Scarborough dau.of William
25 Mar.1789,	Elliot,	George	Mary Merritt,(O.B.XV;116)
25 July 1770,		" Jr.	Mary Merrit, Richard Elliott's consent

17 March 1815, Elliott, George   to   Mary Ann Walker dau.of Alexander W.dec'd

24 Dec.1814,   "   Martha A.E. Walker

25 Feb.1798,   John   * * * Maclin dau.of Thomas (W.B.VI;143)

24 Aug.1824,   Robert   Minerva G.Hill

24 Mar.1788,   William   Mary Jameson, Griffin Stith sec.

23 Mar.1789,   "   Martha Merritt (O.B.XV; 116)

 4 July 1762,   * * *   Martha Embry dau.of Henry.(W.B.IV;359)

11 July 1833   Ellis,   John   Eliz.Johnson dau.of N.

27 Sept.1776,   Joseph   Selah Jordan, Batte Peterson sec.

13 Apr.1829,   Tatnai   Lucy Petillo

 8 April 1844,   William J.   Catherine E.White

28 June 1830,   Wyatt   Emily Hampton

19 Dec.1829,   Elmore,   Anderson   Pulcheria Moore dau.of Francis

14 Mar.1807,   James   Polly Pritchett

22 Nov.1850,   "   Martha Barnes

24 Jan.1791,   Jesse of Char.   Ann Bran, dau.of James sec.

25 Dec.1820,   William   Susan K.Barnes dau.of James

23 Dec.1771,   Emmerson,   Rev.Arthur   Ann Nevison wid.of Rev.John (O.B.XI;430)

13 May 1768,   Emmery   * * *   Mary Bass dau.of James.(W.B.IV,80)

16 Dec.1822,   Ennis,   John   Nancy C.Hawkins dau.of Smart

13 Sept.1841,   Enroughty,   John   Ann Grammer

15 Dec.1845,   Epperson,   Henry N.   Pamelia Ann Scoggin

27 Sept.1817,   James   Martha M.Pritchett dau.of Moses

 3 Sept.1845,   James Jr.   Eliz.S.Smith

10 April 1840, Eppes,   Benjamin F.   Ann E.Field

23 Nov.1795,   Richard   Sarah Mathis, James Mathis sec.

10 Nov.1843, Epes,   Richard   to   Francis Jane Dunn

12 Dec.1788, Etter,   John   Mary King dau.of Henry, Jesse Felts
                                                                      sec.
 4 Jan.1790,   * *   Molly Betsey King dau.of Henry(W.B.V;
                                                                      298)
28 Sept.1818,Evans,   Coleman   Martha Shell

18 Dec.1810,   David L.   Polly Wyche

13 Jan.1786,   Francis   Eliz. Wade wid.,Anamanus Abernathy sec.

 3 Dec.1808,   "   Eliza L.Bottom

23 Dec.1820,   George   Vincey Parish

22 Mar.1803,   John   Elinor Hughes Owen

26 May 1757,   Mathew   Rebecca Scoggin dau.of William.(W.B.III;
                                                                      217)
19 Aug.1836,   Stephen   Mary N.Moore

21 Dec.1778,   Williams   Rebecca Braton

29 Sept.1788,(Apr.1770)William   Eliz.Brodnax dau.of William & Ann.(W.B.
                                                                      V;285)
22 Dec.1794, Ezell,   Davis   Nancy Davis, John Davis sec.

 4 Nov.1797,   Jeremiah   Susanna Ezell, Herbert Hill sec.

28 Feb.1828,   John A.   Julia Hawkins dau.of Smart

30 July 1796,   Thomas   Nancy Hill, Herbert Hill sec.

 8 May.1811,   Wyatt M.   Polly D.Ezell

21 Jan.1786,   * * *   Tabitha Thrower dau.of Hezekiah(W.B.V;
                                                                      213)
28 Nov.1792,Faircloth, Thomas   Mary Thornton dau.of William.(O.B.XVI,28

11 Jan.1812,Farler,   Henry   Maria M.Andrews

26 Jan.1825,   *   Mary Ann Turbeville dau.of Dorothy

 4 Aug.1841,Farmer,   John   Mary L.Watts

 2 Nov.1791,Featherston,William   Caty Brann, James Brann sec.

 5 Oct.1803,Fennell,   James C.   Betsey Hobbs

28 Feb.1815, Fenner, Robert   to   Lucy M.Saunders

21 Dec.1835, Ferguson, Henry C.   Martha Bishop

3 Apr.1813,   Horatio   Susanna Hamblett, Turner Hamblett wit.

20 Oct.1793,   * * *   Framcina Ingram dau.of John.(W.B.V;520)

3 Jan.1799, Ferrell Hutchins   Mary Pennington dau.of Anney

21 July 1824,Field, Andrew   Agness B.Wyall

16 Apr.1790,   Edmund   Mary Stith dau.of DruryEdward Birchett sec.

15 June 1800,   George   Eliz.B.Stith ,David and Nancy E.Meade wit.

19 Sept.1783,   Theophilis   Martha Simmons wid.,Richard Elliott sec.
                  of Pr.Geo.
22 July 1785   "   Martha Stith exx.of Thomas.O.B.XIV;197)

19 Sept.1783,   Theophilus Jr. Ann Brodnax dau.of Ann ⌊& William dec.⌋
                  of Pr.Geo.
17 Feb.1794,   Dr.Richard   Ann Meade dau.of Andrew, Richard Stith sec.

3 June 1807,   Richard   Sally Edmunds

27 Dec.1818,   " W.   Ann C.Wyatt ward of Thomas Booth

14 Jan.1748,   * * *   Susanna Vaughan dau.of Richard(W.B.II;165)

29 Dec.1780, Fielding, James   Mary Slate wid.,dau.of John Davis.

31 Aug.1810, Finch,   Edward   Jensey Nanny

22 Dec.1789,   George   Nancy Harrison Ivie, Benjamin Jr.sec.

25 June 1821,   Gray   Henrietta Rawlings

24 Dec.1838,   Riley   Emmaline Moore dau.of Marcus.

23 Mar.1821,   William   Sally Moore

21 Dec.1838, Finix,   Edward   Sally Thomason dau.of Banister

10 May 1826, Firth,   Thomas B.   Lucretia A.Wilkes dau.of Mary G.

23 Mar.1795,   William   Sally Rawlings dau.of Henry

25 Jan.1796,   "   Nancy Crowder, John Duggar sec.

28 Dec.1802,   "   Patsey Buchana.

```
28 Oct.1801, Fisher,  Benjamin,     to Nancy Dance
25 Dec.1820,          James            Rebecca A.Barnes dau.of James
23 Nov.1818,          John             Naomi Barnes dau.of James
 1 Oct.1805,            "              Ann Stith wid., Richard Stith sec.
 2 Oct.1806,          William          Polly Cheely dau.of Joseph & Winifred
 4 Jan.1790, Fitzhugh, Richard         Susanna Meade dau.of Andrew,Griffin S.sec.
10 May 1847, Fleshood, William         Harriet Buckley dau.of Francis
 6 Oct.1793, Fletcher,John(Nathan?)    Middleton Myrick sister of  Owen.(W.B.V;
                                                                  571 &590)
28 Jan.1828,          " J.             Lucy C.B.Fletcher
 3 Aug.1842, Flinn,   William          Elvira Sturdivant
24 Nov.1800, Floyd,   Allen            Sally L.Bottom
29 Oct.1772,          Charles          Martha Davis, Nathaniel Robinson sec.
14 Nov.1831,          Fletcher         Eliz.Mathis
26 Jan.1795,          James            Ann Nipper, Jesse Taylor sec.
12 Jan.1832,            "              Eliz.J.Floyd
21 Aug.1802,          Jordan           Frances Capel
 9 Nov.1797,          Morris           Sally Floyd, John Floyd sec.
 7 Dec.1801,          Wells            Eliz.Harrison
28 Oct.1816,          William          Clarissa Miller
24 Feb.1772,          Zachariah        Ann Jones dau.of John Robert
30 Dec.1818,            "              Christian Stegall dau.of George
23 May 1796, Fort,    Arthur           Polly Finch dau.of William & Tabitha.
14 Dec.1799,          Edward           Lucy Lane
23 Apr.1810, Foster,  Beverley         Nancy Ragsdale
28 Dec.1795,          John H.          Celia Lightfoot, John Lightfoot sec.
22 Jan.1798,          "    "           Sally Braswell, William Ward sec.
```

22 Feb.1803,	Foster,	Peter R.	to Sally James dau.of John and Sally
8 Feb.1790,	Fowler,	Briggs	Molly Chambliss, James Pennington sec.
10 Dec.1798,		Mills	Rebecca Redding
19 Feb.1805,	Fox,	Lark	Eliz.Gholson dau.of Thomas
2 Dec.1742,		Richard	Hannah Williamson dau.of John(D.B.II; 204)
14 May 1831,	Fraser,	Edward	Dolly W.Cheely
10 Feb.1844,		Edwin	Mary Chieves Rives
24 Dec.1800,		John	Martha Brown
19 Dec.1836,	Frear,	John D.	Mary P.Peterson dau.of Hannah
25 Nov.1783,	Freeman,	Arthur	Nancy Malone, James Johnson sec.
31 Jan.1797,		Hamlin D.	Betsey Hartwell, Herbert Hill sec.
24 Jan.1774,		Hartwell	Eliz.Baley, William Clack sec.
2 Dec.1842,		Hezekiah	Mary A.Hawthorn dau.of John
26 Aug.1833,		Ruffin	Martha J.Mangum
22 Feb.1819,		Samuel	Betsy Walker
21 Jan.1786,		* * *	Batty Thrower dau.of Hezekiah.(W.B.V;213)
30 Oct.1787,	Ferguson	Edward	Eliz.Hunter, Isaac Roe Walton sec.
19 Dec.1849,	Garland,	Robert C.	Lucy Jane Robins dau.of Solomon
27 May 1771,		Samuel	Eliz.Edmunds dau.of Nicholas
27 Mar.1786,	Garner,	Presley	Betsey Avent, William Avent sec.
28 Mar.1780,		William	Lucy Johnson, William Goodrum sec.
26 Mar.1787,		"	Mary Samford, William K.Samford sec.
13 Sept.1832,	Grammar,	John J.	Maria E.Meade dau.of Richard K. decd.
26 Oct.1799,	Garratt,	Humphrey	Susanna Pritchett
2 Jan.1789,		Mason	Winifred Beckwith Miskell dau.of Daniel & Ann.

20 Nov.1837, George, James   to   Ermine   Thomason dau.of Banister

21 May 1763, Gee,   Charles   Eliz.   Doby dau.of William(W.B.IV;109)

25 Sept.1837,   Jesse   Martha E.C.Rose

15 Apr.1794,   Lucas   Lucy Pennington dau.of S., Benj.Bugg sec

15 Dec.1801,   William   Susan Atkins dau.of Richard & Rebecca.

22 Dec.1808,   Wilson   Rebecca Turbyfield

3 Mar.1762,   * * *   Tabitha Ingram dau.of John (W.B.Iv; 376)

31 Aug.1769, Gholson Thomas   Jeanny Perry, Mark Johnson sec.

3 May 1798,   William   Mary Saunders

6 July 1780, Gibbons, Edward   Mary Maclin, Ben.Goodrich sec.

13 Sept.1812,Gibbs, Henry   Mary Jarrott dau.of David

23 Jan.1804,   John   Patsy Wray

8 Jan.1849,   Joseph F.   Rebecca Rawlings dau.of Rebecca

7 Nov.1784,   Williams   Eliz.Ward, James Wesson sec.

28 Feb.1838,   William E.   Clary Ann Hawkins

14 Jan.1801, Giles, John   Sally Lanier

22 June 1829,Gill,   William   Lucy L.Nolly

12 Feb.1774, Gilliam, * * *   Eliz.Webb dau.of Eliz.

23 Oct.1826, Glidewell,Henry   Eliz.Underhill

17 Nov.1770, Glover, * * *   Eliz.Nance dau.of William

25 Apr.1816, Goode, Alexander   Sarah Worthington

14 Jan.1828,   "   Minerva J.Harrison

31 Mar.1785,   John   Martha Simmons, Andrew Meade sec.

28 July 1828,   Samuel   Mary E.Price

25 May 1789, Goodrich, Benjamin   Tabitha Hicks, Robert Rivers sec.

20 Nov.1799   "   Nancy S.Claiborne

3 Feb.1807,	Goodrich,	Edmund	to	Eliz.B.Goodrich
13 Dec.1825,		George B.		Mary Greene
4 Mar.1800,		Thomas		Eliz.Warwick, William Warwick sec.
5 July 1765,		William		Ann Chapman admx.of John.(O.B.IX;308.)
9 Dec.1797,		* * *		Mary Camp (W.B.VI;132)
23 Nov.1801,	Goodrum,	James		Polly Justice
27 Nov.1797,		John		Rebecca Parham, Mordecai Jones sec.
30 Dec.1781,		Thomas		Jane Johnson
30 Mar.1760,		William		Hannah Connelley, Bennett Goodrum sec.
15 Nov.1834,	Goodwyn	Albert F.		Amelia Meade
9 Dec.1803,		Armistead		Sarah Dance
27 Apr.1789,		Esau		Patsy C.Tucker dau.of David
7 May 1814,		Francis		Helen Stith dau.of Drury
12 Oct.1770,		James		Judith Thweatt dau.of Judith
7 May 1819,		"		Mary Ann H.Talley dau.of Nancy
20 Oct.1791,		John		Ann Collier, James Peterson sec.
25 Dec.1797,		" Jr.		Lucy Green dau.of Dolly, John Green sec.
27 Nov.1820,		Thomas		Eliz.Fisher
28 S ept.1787,	Gordon,	Abner		Rebecca Ivie dau.of William.B.Ivie sec.
2 Aug.1840,	Grain,	George W.		Martha Smith
3 Apr.1788,	Grant,	* * *		Faithy Fearson dau.of Charles (W.B.V;342)
3 Apr.1788,		* * *		Charlotte Fearson dau.of Charles " " "
5 Nov.1825,		James H.		Rebecca W.Sims dau.of Richard.
31 Mar.1787,	Grantham,	* * *		Eliz.Rawlings dau.of William(W.B.V;202)
6 Sept.1832,	Gray,	Logan		Tabitha G.Alley

23 Feb.1839, Gray,	Seneca	to	Nancy E.Walton
28 Mar.1825,	"		
			Martha Walton
13 Oc t.1786,	William		Mary Ledbetter dau.of Henry, David Hyde sec.
19 Mar.1840, Grayson,	Thomas		Ann K.Watts
27 Sept.1819,Graves,	"		Patsy Roberts dau.of Abraham.
6 June 1809,	William		Martha Smith widow
9 May 1838,	" H.		Emily A.Smith
25 Sept.1786,Green,	Alexander		Sarah Atkins dau.of John deceased.
23 Apr.1815,	Allen		Martha Thrower dau.of Christopher
24 Jan.1783,	Clement		Frances Parham orphan of William,F.Green sec.
11 Feb.1822,	"		Lucy Goodrich
7 Apr.1835,	Daniel M.		Levinia Blankenship
7 Aug.740,	Edward		Burchet Turner wid. of Joseph.(O.B.1;335)
23 Jan.1779,	Frederick		Frances Crittenden, Henry Crittenden wit.
27 Mar.1845,	George W.		Rebecca A.Branch
25 Apr.1781,	James		Betsey Bass dau.of Thomas, Roger Mallory sec.
5 Dec.1772,	John of Amelia		Dolly Jones dau.of John Robin
23 Apr.1792,	Mark		Ann barbar Claiborne, Thomas Claiborne sec.
14 Dec.1797,	"		Patsy Harwell
20 Mar.1822,	"		Sally H.Powell
3 June 1808,	Myhill		Nancy Jackson
23 Apr.1810,	Nathaniel		Lucy Richardson
23 Oct.1786,	Peter		Dolly Foster dau.of Anthony,Jas.W.Green sec.
30 Mar.1829,	Robert H.		Mary P.Green
24 Sept.1787,	Sterling		Ann Eaves, Jesse Freeman sec.

* * * 1779,	Green,	William	to * * *
23 Apr.1841,		"	Mary F.Jones dau.of T.Jones
9 April 1856,		* * *	Eliz.Bass dau.of Thomas (W.B.V;168)
26 Jan.1789,	Greenhill,	Joseph	Patsey Stainback, William Stainback sec.
12 Feb.1828,	Gregory,	John W.	Jane W.Jones dau.of Mary T.
12 Oct.1842,		Joseph S.	Ann E.Stith dau.of Obediah
22 Sept.1842,		Richard C.	Sally M.Stith
24 Feb.1772,	Gresham,	Anthony	Eliz.Ingram exx.of James)O.B.XI;501)
8 July 1816,		John	Tabitha J.Collier
10 Nov.1827,		William	Jane B.Hudson
25 Dec.1802,	Grigg,	Charles	Priscilla Cheely
29 Mar.1760,	Grimes,	George	Hannah Collier dau.of Thomas (W.B.III;335)
22 June 1801,		John	Rebecca Meskell
4 Sept.1849,	Griffin,	John T.	Martha Ann Sills dau.of Joshua
16 Dec.1833,		Nicholas	Ann Overby dau.of Thomas
25 Nov.1839,		Sabat	Eliz.M.Short dau.of Griffin
22 Nov.1824,		Samuel	Mary J.Wesson dau.of Isaac
12 Apr.1815,		Wright	Nancy G.Rawlings
16 May 1793,	Grubbs,	Hickerson	Caty Hailey dau.of Thomas, John Hailey sec.
2 Sept.1816,		Thomas	Lucy D.Brown
19 Dec.1807,	Gunn,	Dudley	Sarah Tillman
11 July 1812,		" G.	Rebecca D.Ryland
8 Nov.1825,		Freeman J.	Maria Bridgforth
13 Sept.1797,		Radford	Silvey Read, Peter Read sec.
29 Nov.1848,		Samuel H.	Martha Daniel dau.of Peter
20 June 1769,		* * *	Hannah White dau.of Samuel(W.B.IV;56)

12 May,1756, Hagood,	John	to Lucy Rawlings, dau.of William
11 Apr.1808,	Richard	Sally R.Smith
31 Mar.1787,	* * *	Hannah Rawlings dau.of William (W.B.V;202)
31 Mar.1787,	* * *	Lucy Rawlings dau.of William " " " "
28 May,1770, Hailey	Henry	Letitia Hyde of N.C.,age by M.Johnson.
29 Nov.1781,	Robert	Polly Crook dau.of George, Moses Dobbins sec.
26 Dec.1796,	Sterling	Liddy Ross, William Trotter sec.
10 Aug.1849, Hall	Benjamin B.	Martha J.Rawlings dau.of Mary R.
23 Nov.1778,	Durham	Frances Hicks, Lewis Hicks sec.
5 Jan.1775,	Dyson,	Ann Hunt, Thomas Rivers sec.
22 Nov.1802,	Edward	Eliz.Kelly
23 May 1814,	"	Claremon Morris dau.of Robert
14 Feb.1816,	James	Rebecca Sammonds
23 May 1818,	Richard	Sarah Smith
21 Mar.1797, Halsey,	James	Susanna Ingram
25 Feb.1791, Hamblen,	William	Poly Jennings Fowlkes, Bennett Goodrum sec.
29 Aug.1779, Hamilton	* * *	Tabitha Thweatt (W.B.V;73)
27 Sept.1830,Hamlett,	Turner	Lucy Ann Ogburn dau.of Sarah
25 Feb.1791, Hamlin,	William	Polly G.Fowlkes dau.of Thomas
2 June 1845,	" C.	Vespena E.Jones
22 Dec.1843, Hammock,	Hugh	Martha R.Bishop
18 Nov.1764,	* *	Ann Lambert dau.of Hugh (W.B.III;426)
18 Nov.1764,	* *	Mildred Lambert dau.of Hugh," " "
2 Oct.1832, Hammon,	William	Jane C.Rawlings
22.Dec.1813, Hammond,	"	Mary Barrow.
21 Dec.1841, Hammons,	James T.	Mary Jane Floyd

44

24 Dec.1833, Hammons,	Thomas E.	to	Martha E.Lanier dau.of Mary S.
29 July 1789,Hammonds,	* * *		Mildred Morris dau.of Thomas(W.B.V;324)
17 Dec.1814, Hampton,	Ambrose S.		Polly Slate dau.of Randolph
13 Dec.1803,	David		Betsey Browder
29 Jan/1807,	Jeremiah		Eliz.Allen
13 Dec.1800,	William		Patsey Potts
19 Mar.1792, Hamour,	Mark		Tabitha Hamour dau.of John.John Taylorr sec.
3 Apr.1778, Hancock,	* *		Sally Stainback dau.of Francis(W.B.V;57)
27 Feb.1804,	Francis		Martha James
23 Dec.1811,	"		Eliz.House
15 Dec.1791,	Henry		Dolly Rawlings, Richard Rece sec.
25 April 1831,Hanks,	Thomas		Ann Reece
5 Aug.1831, Hardaway,	Frederick M.		Mary C.S.Maclin,
25 Mar.1816,	George		Margaret Drummond dau.of John
11 Oct.1803,	Henry S.		Susan Lundie
2 Apr.1810,	James H.		Eliza M.G.Raines
26 Jan.1774,	John		Mary Sexton, Joseph Lett sec.
21 Feb.1788,	" Sr.		Eliz.Maclin dau.of Col.Frederick
18 Dec.1820,	" C.		Mary H.Harwell dau.of John H.
3 June 1796,	John		* * Stith dau.of Thomas Sr.(W.B.VI;356)
1 Nov.1783,	Robert of Din.Co.Sarah Hicks dau.of James Sr(or Joseph?)		
7 Nov.1817,	" S.		Maria E.Drummond
* July 1785,	Thomas		Rebecca Powell
7 Nov.1793,	"		* * * Simmons dau.of Susanna(W.B.V;521)
22 Oct.1784,	William,Capt.		Eliz.Hicks dau.of James
1 Mar.1813,	"		Ann J.S.Lundie

17 Dec.1818, House,	Hartwell	to	Nancy Harrison
9 May 1816,	Henry		Eliz.J.Owen dau.of Robert
16 May 1820,	"		Lucy S.Owen
19 Dec.1837,	" A.		Martha C.House
4 Jan.1745,	Isaac		Mary Mattox (O.B.II; 129)
3 Feb.1810	"		Eliz.Kelley
27 Nov.1828,	"		Martha D.Rawlings
24 Dec.1798,	" Flood		Eliz.Neal
16 Oct.1836,	" F.		Eliz.Dromgoole
9 Feb.1735,	James		* * Mattocks dau.of William.(Vol.1;175)
5 Dec.1803,	John		Keziah Wesson
21 Feb.1775,	"		Eliz.Sims aged 21, John Blanks sec.
18 Jan.1842,	" E.		Mary E.Quarles
24 Dec.1824,	" J.		Mary Phipps
19 Dec.1835,	Jordan		Martha J.Mason
21 Dec.1807,	Joseph		Sinthey Wray, dau.of Reuben
11 Dec.1841,	Laban		Eliz.Barnes
25 Feb.1771,	Lawrence		Lucy Hobbs, John Hobbs sec.
22 Jan.1779,	Philip		Nancy Collier, Myhill Collier sec.
8 Dec.1848,	Robert S.		Mary E.Owen
13 Dec.1796, Howse,	Isham		Betsy Gee, Burwell Lanier sec.
24 Feb.1784, Howard,	Mordecai,		Jane Anderton dau.of Isaac.
25 Jan.1791,	Richard		Eliz.Anderton, John Rose Williams sec.
22 Dec.1789,	Thomas		Betsey Ledbetter dau.of Jean.
20 Dec.1847,	William G.		Catherine E.Moore
2 Dec.1820, Howell, Spencer			Eliz.M.Talley

15 Oct.1808, Howerton,	Drury	to	Betsy Biggs,
6 Jan.1846,	James W.		Elvy E.Hawkins
26 Nov.1832,	" "		Eliz.P.Lanier
24 May,1841,	Richard A.		Susan J.Turbeville
30 Aug.1830,	Thomas H.		Ann J.Williams
24 Mar.1791,	William		Martha Traylor, Benj.Roper sec.
27 Nov.1786, Hubbard,	John		Mary Gresham, Ap Gresham sec.
18 June 1827,	William		Ann Rawlings
1 July 1844,Huckstep,	Jesse		Evelina T.Wesson dau.of Green
21 Dec.1846, Hudgins,	John H.		Mary J.Walker
5 Apr.1788,	Samuel,		* * Lanier dau.of Nicholas (W.B.V;466)
4 July 1802,Hudson,	Gregory		Bridgett Davis
5 Dec.1817,	Joseph G.		Lucetta Julia Seward dau.of John
9 Jan.1844,	William W.		Harriet J.Jones
3 April 1840,Huff,	Daniel		Priscilla H.Steed
9 Nov.1793,	James,		Rebecca Moseley, Samuel Moseley sec.
26 July 1797,	"		Sarah Gunn dau.of William(W.B.VI;118)
8 Dec.1823,	"		Judith C.Birdsong
2 Oct.1844,	"		Louisa B.Heartwell
24 Nov.1793,	Joseph		Keziah Christie, John Phenix sec.
24 Dec.1796,	Julius		Huldah Moseley dau.of Samuel
12 Dec.1796,	Lundie		Pharaby Read
3 Aug.1799,	"		Sarah White dau.of Blewmer
27 Apr.1789,	Thomas		Tabitha Huff,Mary Huff's consent.
30 Apr.1813,	William		Nancy Huff
4 May 1765, Hughes,	William		Sarah Hightower wid.of Charnel.(O.B.IX; 242)

4 Mar.1833, Hunnicutt, James E.P.   to Martha L.Atkinson dau.of John

13 Aug.1834, Hunt   Etheldred J.   SydneyHJ.Owen

26 Dec.1769,   Judkins   Martha Batte,William Batte's consent

25 July 1768,   Thomas   Athelia Morris

 4 Oct.1832,   " P.   Ann M.Field

31 Jan.1778,   Turner   Ann Stainback dau.of Francis,Thos.Rivers
                                                                      sec.
30 May 1826, Hurt,   James B.   Eliza A.B.Jones dau.of Mary T.

17 Mar.1834,   " M.   Eliz.D.Davis

21 Dec.1838, Huskey,   "   Martha W.Wesson dau.of Washington

15 Oct.1779, Hutchins,   Charles   Patty Green, Edward Jones sec.

17 May 1797, Hutt,   Thomas B.   Eliz.Bennett

17 May 1778, Hyde,   * * *   Rebecca Warren dau.of Benj.(W.B.V;18)

30 Nov.1803, Ingram,   Bartholomew   Eliz.Dunnington

20 Dec.1802,   Benjamin   Susanna H.Manson dau.of Thomas

29 Mar.1808,   "   Sally Mason

26 Mar.1804,   Henry   Eliz.Overby

 4 Apr.1744,   John   Ann Sisson dau.of Thomas (D.B.II;470)

24 Dec.1811,   "   Mary Watson

13 Nov.1790,   Thomas   Mary Ann Ingram, Chs.Harris sec.

27 Sept.1802,   "   Sally P.Hunnicutt

23 Nov.1812,   William   Nancy Morris

13 Feb.1819, Irby,   " B.   Sarah W.Stith dau.of Ahn

 2 Nov.1769, Irvine,   Bedford   Frances Jones, Mordecai Jones sec.

23 Dec.1807, Ives,   James   Celia H.Lafoon

23 July 1806, Ivey,   Hardiman S.   Eliz.Bass dau.of Parlin

48

2 Jan.1799, Ivey,   Thomas to Catherine Connell dau.of William

21 Mar.1815, Ivie   Benjamin,   Eliz.Williams

13 July 1816,   "   Eliz.Jackson

2 Nov.1812,   Sterling   Betsey R.Ivie

28 May 1787, Ivey   Benjamin   Jane Woodrough dau.of George, B.Ezell sec.

* * * 1821 Ivy,   Lewis   Eliz.Moore

8 Feb.1791 Jackson,   Allen   Sally Scarbrough dau.of Lewis

7 Dec.1825,   Asbury   Sally Doyal

20 Nov.1810   Burwell   Nancy Baugh, Littleberry Baugh sec.

17 Sept.1834,   "   A.   Eliz.Birthright

10 Jan.1809,   Coleman   Frances Richardson dau.of Jordan

23 Dec.1793,   David   Martha Edwards ward of Jno.Hardaway.

5 June 1798,   "   Polly Mason

11 Sept.1837,   "   Mary E.Rawlings dau.of Peterson

27 May 1833,   Frederick S.Margaret S.Gee

17 Nov.1836,   George B.   Susanna S.Noble

5 Sept.1807,   Green   Rebecca R.Lucas

24 Feb.1772,   Henry   Ann Mabry dau.of Hinchia(O.B.XI;459)

21 Dec.1784,   "   Ann Brodnax dau.of Ann

27 Dec.1825,   "   Eliz.P.Parham

25 July 1831,   "   Rebecca Mangum dau.of Winifred.

15 April 1819,   James   Harriet A.Duggar dau.of Richmond

6 Aug.1746,   John   Eliz.Loyd dau.of Thomas(D.B.III;305)

21 Dec.1824,   "   Susan Crittenden

18 Aug.1840,   " G.   Martha A.E.Gee

49

25 Nov.1793,	Harding,	Abraham	to	Sylvia Price, Joel Price sec.
13 Feb.1804,	Hardy,	Charles		Sally G.Green dau.of Dolly
21 Nov.1840,		Elisha		Mary Ann Sturdivant
22 July 1833,		John C.		Emmeline T.Eldridge
28 Apr.1827,		Larkin		Ann M.Palmer dau.of W.
6 Feb.1809,		Vincent		Sally Penn
22 Nov.1814,	Harp,	Manning		Betty Mitchell, William Tarpley sec.
22 Dec.1794,	Harper,	Benjamin		Anna Mathis dau.of Mathew
25 Aug.1800		"		Nancy Ingram dau.of John
22 Dec.1778,		Joseph of Din.Co.		Eliz.Lambert, Hugh Williams sec.
17 May 1844,		" W.		Sarah J.Moore
11 Feb.1797,		Nathaniel		Polly Fisher
28 Jan.1794,		* * ⚹		Mary Ingram dau.of Benjamin
27 Aug.1821,	Harris,	Ambrose,		Francis Williams dau.of Nancy
* May 1752,		Arthur		Eliz.Douglas dau.of John (O.B.IV;188)
13 Dec.1779,		Bowler		Nancy Kemp Goodrich, Briggs Goodrich sec.
27 Sept.1813,		David		Susanna Tatum
27 June 1774,		Etheldred		Eliz.Warren, Moses Harris sec.
16 July 1770,		Gideon		* * * Warren, Edward T ** sec.
2 May 1780,		James		Chrictian Harrison., Willis Wills sec.
7 Dec.1840,		" N.		Caroline M.Orgain
17 Dec.1818,		John		Sally Wright
16 June 1801,		Kinchen		Mary J.C.Chapman
25 Dec.1809,		Larkin		Polly Lightfoot
5 Nov.1741,		Nathan		Catherine Walton dau.of George)O.B.II; 50)

50

20 Nov.1793, Harris,	Robert,	to	Eliz.Seward Clayton, John Clayton sec.
12 Aug.1813,	"		Rebecca Rice, William & Rebecca Rice con
23 Jan.1826,	" H.		Martha M.Howell dau.of S.
21 Mar.1823,	" P.		Mary A.E.Rice
23 Feb.1818,	Samuel M.		Sally Vaughan
28 Aug.1771,	Sterling		Ann Adams, (O.B.XI;405)
* Mar.1774,	"		" " (O.B.XII;514)
18 Jan.1802,	"		Sylvia Lane.
22 Nov.1831,	William E.		Rebecca G.Powell
27 Aug.1833,	" H.		M.A.J.Morris dau.of Richard B.
4 Oct.1773,	* * *		Eliz.Collier dau.of Charles.
17 May.1778,	* * *		Rita Warren dau.of Benjamin
13 Dec.1802, Harrison	Benjamin		Silvia Bass
25 Apr.1808,	"		Polly Lashley
25 May 1801,	Charles,		Betsey Gladish
29 Jan.1778,	Cuddy		Eliz.Harrison, Gabriel Harrison sec.
17 Dec.1825,	Edward		Ann R.Dixon dau.of John
7 Oct.1830,	Edmund		Ann Malone wadr of Edmund Harrison
31 Dec.1810,	Gabriel		Sally Short.
24 Sept.1849,	George W.		Sarah M.Tucker
7 Jan.1786,	Ishmael		Eliz.Gee, Thomas Rivers sec.
18 July 1822,	James		Sarah Hall widow
13 Nov.1759,	"		Sarah Collier dau.of William (W.B.III;324)
22 Nov.1830,	"		Eliz.Coley
4 Jan.1745,	John		* * Mattox (O.B.II;129)
14 Dec.1779,	"		Cresey Steed dau.of Winifred widow.

5 Nov.1799, Harrison	John	to	Dorothy Hancock, Harrison Hartwell sec.
22 Nov.1815,	"		Nancy Pearson
24 Nov.1808,	"		Polly Hicks
23 Aug.1836,	" W.		Mary Ann C.Trotter
18 June 1845,	Jones J.		Virginia A.C.A?Delbridge dau.of Benj.
26 Oct.1807,	Joseph		Anthanico Hancock
1 Sept.1809,	Mark		Mary Olive Whitby
5 Nov.1825,	Mortimer		Manerva J.Rawlings dau.of James
17 Nov.1794,	Nathaniel		Eliz.White dau.of Blumer, Stephen White sec.
25 Mar.1799,	"		Martha K.Brodnax
25 May 1801,	"		Rebecca Cook
3 Nov.1815,	"		Mary Birdsong
12 Nov.1798,	Peter		Catherine Boswell, William Boswell sec.
7 Dec.1837,	Smith		Harriet A?Turbyfill
24 May 1790,	Thomas		Mary Love dau.of Hugh, Thos,Washington sec.
27 Nov.1826,	" G.		Eliz.Delbridge
* May 1759,	William		Ann Major, John Edmundson sec.
23 Dec.1782,	"		Eliz.Boswell wid.of William.
26 Mar.1787,	"		Patty Jones, Harwood Clary sec.
23 Aug.1790,	"		* * Clary dau.of Harweed.(W.B.V;321)
27 Nov.1797,	"		Tabitha Parham
16 Feb.1773,	* * *		Joany Brown dau.of Richard.(W.B.IV;148)
11 Oct.1796,	* * *		Eliza Gee dau.of William (W.B.VI;73)
2 Mar.1799,	William		Eliz.Tilman dau.of Elizabeth.
22 Aug.1831,	"		Eliza S.Judd
7 Sept.182o,	" C.		Rebecca Dromgoole

52

25 Nov.1811, Harrison,	William H.	to	Ann Williams
11 Dec.1832,	" J.		Mary E.Parish dau.of Sally E.Dugger
29 Oct.1835,	" T.		Lucy Ann Buckley dau.of Frances
5 Jan.1802,	Willie		Nellie Holloway
26 May 1759,	* * *		Ann Major
12 Oct.1795,	Benj.		Sally Cole, Thomas Harrison sec.
26 Dec.1796, Hartwell	Armistead		Martha Gholson, Andrew Tarver sec.
27 Jan.1817,	Edmund		Eliza C.Warwick
27 May 1819	Harrison		Rebecca Lightfoot
24 Feb.1806,	Lett S.		Sally Woodroff
5 Aug.1771,	Richard		Susanna Stainback dau.of Francis
27 Feb.1775, Harvey,	John		Patty Ivey, Thomas Ivey sec.
25 Jan.1791,	Rawleigh		Rainey Brittle , Triford Harvey sec.
7 Jan.1822,	Thomas		Eliz.Thompson
8 Feb.1788,	Triford		Sraah Brittle, Arad Walton sec.
22 Nov.1802, Harwell,	Absalom		Rebecca Williams,
29 Jan.1827,	Alfred		Eliz.H.Bass
21 Dec.1803,	Hartwell		Tempe Edwards
16 Nov.1779,	James		Rebecca Barner, Henry Bishop sec.
24 Dec.1796,	Nathaniel		Susanna Westmoreland, Peter Williams sec
5 Feb.1784,	Francis		Eliz.Loftin dau.of John, James Smith "
5 Feb.1784,	Harbert		Ann Westmoreland dau.of Thomas decd.
16 Apr.1805,	Richard		Nancy Owen
11 Mar.1808,	" M.		Mary Atkinson dau.of Sarah
2 Sept.1741,	Samuel		* * * Jackson dau.of Ambrose(D.B.II;99)
28 March 1751, Little	"		Abigail Jackson (O.B.IV;39)

27 Feb.1804, Harwell,	Shadrach	to	Ann Harrison
27 Feb.1805,	William		Sally Hicks
7 Oct.1831,	" Sr.		Eliz,H.McKenny
14 June 1745,	* * *		Ann Jackson dau.of Ambrose (W.B.II;109)
23 Sept.1766,	* * *		Sarah Simmons dau.of Peter.(W.B.III;491)
10 Jan.1818, Haskins,	Creed		Ann Meade dau.of Richard W.
30 Dec.1841,	Edward		Ann A.Turnbull
28 Jan.1825,	John		Eliz.C.Haskins
11 Feb.1802,	Robert		Susan Edmunds
12 Jan.1793, Hawkes,	* * *		Mary Daniel dau.of Joseph (W.B.V;550)
25 Dec.1843, Hawkins,	Benjamin E.		Su.E.Williams
* Sept.1747,	John		Mary Wyatt dau.of Henry
21 Dec.1830,	Nathan		Eliz.Barner
* * 179*	Smart		Marian Foart, William Connelly sec.
1 June 1812,Hawthorn,	Bolling		Susan Wynne
28 Dec.1828,	"		Mary Barrow dau.of Dennis
15 Nov.1841,	"		Amanda Brown dau.of Thomas
13 Oct.1816,	Frederick		Nancy Wynne
26 Apr.1815,	John		Susanna Hawthorn
7 Dec.1840,	" A.		Mary E.Kennedy dau.of Jesse
9 Mar.1815,	Micajah		Frances Morriss
15 Aug.1829,	Mitchell		Mary E.Stegall
15 July 1797,	Peter		Mary Ann Oldham
7 Jan.1769,	* * *		* * Weaver dau.of John(W.B.III;530)
23 Sept.1789, Hay,	George		Rebecca Brodnax, Richard Gregory con.
			Thomas Carter sec.
27 Oct.1795, Hayes,	Henry		Polly Clarke, Jones Williams sec.

54

26 Dec.1791, Hayley,	Thomas	to	Nancy Vaughan, Hickerson Grubbs sec.
2 Aug.1794, Haymore,	John		Rebecca Maghe, Mark Haymore sec.
20 Dec.1779, Haymour,	Britain Jones		Susanna Avery dau.of John,Wm.Abernathy sec.
24 Mar.1767, Haynes,	Herbert		Eliz.Downing exx.of William(O.B.X;229)
22 Apr.1782,	Thomas		Frances Stith dau.of William,Jos.Mason sec.
19 Dec.1826, Heagood,	Randolph		Eliza Jane Peebles
18 Dec.1797, Hearn,	John Jr.		Nancy B.Linch
20 Nov.1816, Heath,	Joseph W.		Mary M.Mason widow
19 Aug.1760 Heis,	Tucker		Rebecca Massie dau.of Joseph
28 Oct.1800, Hermon,	George		Nancy Bethshares dau.of Ruth
21 Dec.1790, Hicks,	Benjamin		* * Floyd dau.of Josiah (W.B.V;396)
8 July 1771,	* * *		Judith Collier dau.of Isaac (W.B.IV;80)
29 Dec.1789,	* * *		Nancy Harrison dau.Benj.Sr.(W.B.V;345)
10 Apr.1802,	* * *		Frances Eliz.Bracey dau.of Thomas
5 Oct.1813,	Benjamin H.		Amanda R.James
14 Dec.1844,	" J.		Rebecca B.Hicks dau.of E.B.
23 Feb.1824,	Francis B.		Mary M.Davis dau.of Games
11 Apr.1808,	Hamlin		Jean Powell
22 Apr.1782,	Isaac		Ann Booth dau.of Reuben decd.Binns Jones sec.
26 Nov.1787,	James		Judith Collier dau.of Charles
25 Nov.1771,	John		Ann Harrison dau.of Benjamin
24 Jan.1780,	"		Rachel Williams, David Williams sec.
18 Sept.1810,	"		Nancy Bennet
22 Apr.1799,	Jordan		Lucy Pettit
3 Jan.1814,	Joseph		Milly B.Williams
27 Apr.1807,	Paschal		Lucy Hall

24 Dec.1813, Hicks,   Reuben A.   to   Eliz.S.Lewis dau.of Benjamin

 4 Mar.1726,   Robert   Eliz.Urvin dau.of Eliz. (Vol.1;266)

14 Oct.1813,   Thomas   Lucy G.Lewis dau.of Benjamin

24 Dec.1794,   "   Jean Hampton

22 Feb.1836,   " J.   Lucinda F.Davis

 4 Dec.1834, Higgins,   Daniel   Nancy Lanier

10 Oct.1780, Hill,   Abner   Rebecca Parham dau.of William (W.B.V;113)

23 Dec.1824,   Alfred   Eliza Maclin dau.of Augustine W.

 1 June 1773,   Green,   Mary Seawell, Benj.Seawell sec.

17 Dec.1818,   "   Jane Jackson

25 Mar.1746,   Hamon   Martha Deloach dau.of William(O.B.II;140)

24 Nov.1825,   Richard,Dr.   Anne E.Gholson dau.of William

11 Jan.1781,   Thomas   Frances Smith, Eliz.Smith's consent

25 Mar.1746,   William   Anne Deloach dau.of William (O.B.II;140)

24 Oct.1758,   "   Priscilla Embry wid] of Henry Jr.

27 Sept.1790,   "   Sarah Lanier, Miles Williams sec.

 2 Sept.1844,   " S.   Mary E.Woolsey dau.of Richard D.

 6 Dec.1774,   * * *   Mary Booth dau.of Charles (W.B.IV;249)

20 Dec.1837, Hillard,   Robert C.,Col.   Mary R.H.Walker ward of James W.Cook
             of Nash Co.N.C.
24 Jan.1823, Hightower,Gregory,   Mary Trotter

13 Dec.1771, Hines,   William   Eliz.Turner widow, David Hines sec.

 9 May 1774,   * * *   Ann Donaldson dau.of Benj.C.(W.B.IV;418)

 9 May 1774,   * * *   Sarah "   "   "   " " " "

28 Sept.1818, Hitchcock,Hartwell   Frances P.Atkinson

14 Nov.1814, Hite,   William L.   Eliz.H.Mitchell

21 Nov.1818, Hobbs,   David,Dr.   Mary W.Hinton niece of John H.of Peters-
                                                                          burg

8 Mar.1790, Hobbs,   Frederick   to   Sally Moss dau.of David, Benj.Jackson

18 Dec.1832,   Willie J.   Matilda F.Walton   sec.

* * 1787, Hodge,   John   Jane Thornton

27 Dec.1814, Hogan, Daniel   Eliz.L.Warson

5 Mar.1791, Holmes, Edward   Hannah Mathews, William Mitchell sec.

23 Aug.1766, Holcome, * *   Margaret Durham dau.of George(W.B.III;470

22 June 1816,Holloway,William   Eliz.Kelly

13 Dec.1797, Holmes, Isaac   Frances Parham, John C.Courtney sec.

14 May 1818,   John B.   Ann E.Robertson

25 Oct.1784,   William   Sarah Marriott dau.of Thomas.(W.B.V;316)

15 June 1782,   "   Sarah Warren wid.of John deceased

8 Dec.1787, Holloway,Lewis   Rachel Williams, Roger Williams sec.

23 Dec.1799,   Silas   Abby Moseley

15 Aug.1837,   William   Sarah Parham dau.of Nicholas

29 June 1797,Holobay, Joseph   Lucy Branders

20 Sept.1766,Holt   Thomas of Surry   Eliz.Cocke dau.of Brazure.(W.B.IV;32)

* July 1787,   William   Frances Mabry

9 Dec.1762, Hopkins, * * *   Sarah Williams.(W.B.IV;368)

6 Sept.1817,Horsington,David   Martha S.Carrington dau.of Frances.

25 Mar.1767, Horton, Amos   Jane Ezell dau.of William (O.B.X;280)

24 Jan.1800, House,   Ambrose   Polly Hartwell

23 Dec.1799,   Claiborne   Polly Ledbetter, Isaac Ledbetter sec.

25 Oct.1790,   Drury   Eliz.Nash aged 23, Robert Harrison sec.

7 Feb.1829,   Dudley   Martha G.Lynch

22 Oct.1804,   Green   Betsy Lanier

1 Mar.1823,   Guidford   Rebecca C.White dau.of John

25 Feb.1811, Jackson,	Lewis,	to	Polly Freeman
12 Jan.1822,	Mabry		Sally Delbridge
17 May 1778,	Mark		Martha Warren dau.of Benjamin(W.B.V;18)
27 Feb.1797,	Randle		Rebecca Brett, Epharim Jackson sec.
24 Sept.1769,	Samuel		Mary King dau.of Joseph
27 Sept.1808,	Stephen		Jane Stainback
31 Oct.1825,	" S.		Ann D.Hill
23 June 1828,	Tyree B.		Julia Cheely
12 Oct.1840,	Tyre B.		Martha W.Tucker
26 Dec.1808,	William		Susan Porch
15 Dec.1827,	"		Polly Bradley
29 Sept.1801,	* *		Eliz.Avery dau.of George (W.B.VI;375)
19 Oct.1770,	* *		Sausanna Randle dau.of William(W.B.IV;67)
16 Jan.1773,	* *		Amy Williams dau.of William(W.B.IV;473)
1 Apr.1735, Jacobs,	Thomas		Tabitha Hicks dau.of Robert & Frances. (Vol.1;167)
7 Dec.1819, James,	Allen		Ann C.Wilkinson
23 Dec.1812,	Anderson		Frances House
4 May 1805,	George		Jincy P.Powell
22 Nov.1802,	John		Patsy Hancock dau.of Sarah
30 Oct.1792,	* * *		Eliz.Lenoir dau.of Robert Lanier (W.B.V; 510)
13 Oct.1759 Janes	* * *		Faith Bailey (W.B.III;307)
11 Mar.1779, Jenkins,	Thomas		Eliz.Major, Samuel Major Jr.sec.
23 Oct.1786,	"		Mary Washington dau.of Thomas decd.
28 Aug.1732,	Williams		Ann Naper dau.of Joseph, Vol.1;22)
9 Jan.1834, Jeter,	Albert A.		Susan E.Harrison dau.of James J.
8 Sept.1778,	Andrew		Mary Smith, Eads Smith's consent.

4 Jan.1781, Jeter,	John Jr.	to	Eliz.Tomlinson
29 May 1834,	James S.		Eliza Ann Rawlings
4 Jan.1781,	John Jr.		Eliz.Tomlinson, Edmund Jeter sec.
13 Oct.1804, Jett,	Thomas, Capt.		Frances Starke dau.of Eliz.
20 Jan.1807,	Thornton		Lucy B.Randolph, Robert Jackson sec.
27 Feb.1816,	William		Catherine Batte dau.of William
6 Sept.1849,Johnson,	Alexander		Caroline R.Bowen
28 Nov.1808,	Anderson		Catherine C.Greenhill
26 May 1772,	Benjamin		Isabella Chapman widow, Michael Wallace sec.
21 Jan.1786,	"		Susanna Jackson dau.of Burwell
26 Oct.1835,	" W.		Eliza G.Ogburn dau.of John
16 May 1791,	Charles		Patty Lightfoot 21, William M.Johnson sec.
7 Nov.1796,	David		Betsy L.Hammond, William M.Johnson sec.
24 Feb.1840,	" J.		Jane Barrow dau.of Thomas
26 Nov.1827,	Edward		Minerva W.Stith
26 May 1834,	Fielding		Jane E.Wells dau.of Sally
6 Oct.1797,	George		Nancy Howard (W.B.VI;179)
19 July 1808,	"		Eliz.Croft
11 Aug.1849,	" W.		Frances E.Johnson
14 Sept.1792,	Henry		Milly Wheeler, Thomas Goodrum sec.
30 Dec.1789,	James		Hanna Samford, William Garner sec.
23 Mar.1789,	"		Nancy Wright, James Powell sec.
24 May 1834,	" C.		Mary Bradley
15 Apr.1795,	" Lucas		Nancy Allen, Robert Allen sec.
2 Dec.1806,	Joel		Polly Goodrum
10 June 1817,	John A.		Lucy Ragsdale of Lun.Co.

28 Aug.1848, Johnson,   John H. to   Martha A.Epperson

29 June 1846,   Joseph R.   Louisa J.Howell

 8 May 1801,   Lewis   Lucretia Taylor

16 Dec.1833,   "   Julian Wells dau.of Sally

14 Feb.1849,   "   Mary Saunders dau.of Ann H.

 * Mar.1752,   Moses   Ann Clanton dau.of Edward.(O.B.IV;165)

22 Mar.1749,   Thomas B.   L.Virginia Perkins

26 Jan.1830,   Reuben F.   Louisa A.Jones

16 Feb.1816,   Thomas   Susan Short

24 Aug.1816,   " G.W.   Sarah F.Thomas dau.of Robinson

23 Nov.1807,   William   Nancy Miller

29 Dec.1807,   "   Sally Johnson

 8 Feb.1809,   "   Sarah Hood

29 Nov.1792,   "   Sara McKinney dau.of John(W.B.V;573)

22 Dec.1817,   " M.H.   Rebecca Abernathy

23 Nov.1840,   " " "   Mary Dameron

 2 Dec.1763,   * * *   Mary Fox dau.of William(W.B.IV;387)

16 Jan.1773,   * * *   Ann Williams dau.of William(W.B.IV;473)

23 Oct.1794,   * * *   Susanna Read dau.of William(W.B.V;566)

26 May 1796,   * * *   Martha Mason dau.of Sarah(W.B.VI;57)

29 Sept.1798, Jolly,   Thomas   Susanna Evans

 5 Dec.1848,   William T.   Martha Ann Epes

 6 Feb.1849, Jones   Alfred   Amanda A.Bentley
29 Apr.1771,
29 Apr.1771,   Allan   Rebecca Edwards dau.of Col.Nathaniel
                                      (W.B.IV;84)

17 Dec.1849,   Arthur B.   Sarah A.M.Johnson dau.of Nancy

16 June 1807,   Augustine C. Dianotia Ravenscroft Starke.

25 Feb.1755, Jones	Benjamin to	Lucretia Bryan, Thomas Bryan sec.
23 Nov.1801,	"	Dorothy Mabry
12 Nov.1821,	"	Nancy Haskins dau.of Patty
1 Sept.1800,	Christopher	Martha Keatt dau.of James
10 June 1821,	Daniel	Eliza Worthington
16 July 1803,	David	Betsy Mathews
6 Sept.1793,	Drury of Din.Co.	Martha Simmons dau.of Martha Field
28 Aug.1815,	Enos	Mary Lewis
11 Jan.1799,	Francis	Lucy Simmons, James Field sec.
27 Jan.1806,	Frederick	Sally Maclin
9 Nov.1827,	Green W.	Mary A.E.Prior, Susan P.consent
16 Dec.1786,	Henry	Sally Lightfoot, Thomas Lightfoot sec.
29 Apr.1820,	"	Judith Buckner, Charles Buckner sec.
3 Sept.1835,	" C.	Christiana B.Jones dau.of Robert B.
5 Feb.1842,	" "	Sarah E.Griffin
27 July 1801,	Hicks	Quentena Holloway
13 Jan.1778,	Irwin	Priscilla Dawson dau.of Samuel
18 Oct.1830,	James	Martha Reid
22 July 1849,	" R.	Audney Judd dau.of Thomas
2 June 1787,	John Jr.	Lucy Binns Cergill, Edmunds Stith sec.
20 Dec.1821,	John G.	Sally A.Williams dau.of John
17 May 1756,	Joseph	* * * * *, William Bishop sec.
21 Oct.1803,	Lemuel	Betsy Weaver
10 Dec.1839,	Ravenscroft	Mary Jones Rice
19 Jan.1804,	Reps,	Frances Keatts dau.of Frances
5 July 1824,	Richard S.	Martha H.Pritchett

3 Dec.1821, Jones,	Robert	to	Amanda G.Rawlings
26 Jan.1789,	Samuel		Eliz.Butterill, Burwell Wilkes sec.
22 Oct.1803,	"		Betsey Weaver
30 Sept.1813,	" H.		Ann Lawrence widow.
16 Dec.1833	Squire		Priscilla M.Delbridge
15 Aug.1789,	Stephen		Anna Jones dau.of Thomas of C.Run
16 Aug.1747,	Thomas		Ann Taney dau.of William (O.B.III;243)
8 May 1770,	* * *		Sarah Massey dau.of Ann.(W.B.IV;28)
17 Dec.1804,	Thomas		Polly Burge
25 Dec.1826,	Uriah		Susan Rogers dau.of Joseph
14 Feb.1792,	William of Gr.Co		Agness Bolling Clack, James Clack sec.
31 Mar.1810,	"		Eliz.Wesson
12 July 1813,	"		Charity Seward
2 Dec.1819,	"		Eliz.D.Sims dau.of Richard
20 Dec.1824,	Wilie		Sally Ogburn
22 Feb.1739,	* *		Sarah Jackson dau.of John (O.B.II;127)
23 Aug.1790,	* *		Judith Clary (?)(W.B.V;381)
24 Oct.1781, Jordan,	Arthur		Eliz.Williams widow. George King sec.
21 Apr.1778,	John		Mary Winfield, Edward Winfield sec.
28 Dec.1835,	" F.		Martha E.Ogburn
23 Oct.1815,	Richard,		Eliz.Bridgforth
24 May .770,	* * *		Sarah Peebles dau.of John
15 Dec.1804, Judd,	John		Frances R.Cousins
11 Aug.1832,	"		Martha Eldridge
2 Apr.1836,	Samuel K.		Sally Ann Lucy
16 Dec.1802,	Thomas		Mary Kelly dau.of Samuel

15 July.1835. Judd   Thomas   to Sally Mitchell

 7 May 1793, Justice   Mark   Mary Wesson, Wesson,William cert.to age

27 July 1795,   "   Nelly Wray, John Wray sec.

29 Aug.1798,   William   Rahab Edmunds, Pleasant Smith sec.

26 Sept.1840   "   D.   Sarah Dameron

11 Nov.1799, Keatts,   Henry   Betty Moss dau.of David

 2 Feb.1815, Kelly   David   Martha Woodruff

 4 Jan.1781,   Giles   Jane Constable, Gardner Scoggin sec.

28 July1817   Henry   Rhody Williams

26 Apr.1802,   James J.   Angelica Overby

 3 Sept.1839   "   Eliza A.Thomas dau.of Bennett

 5 Jan.1787,   Jesse   Patsy Phillips dau.of Elizabeth.

22 Dec.1828,   John   Mareah Tatum dau.of Batts

 9 Oct.1830,   "   W   Agnes P.M.J.Brown

19 Nov.1795,   Lewis   Alice Abernathy, William Abernathy sec.

19 Nov.1807,   "   Sarah B.Wilson dau.of John

 9 Dec.1823,   Samuel D.   Mason Abernathy,Mildred Abernathy con.

24 July 1805,   Thomas   Lucy Stith dau.of Thomas

23 Jan.1797,   William   Nancy Penn, Thomas Penn sec.

17 Aug.1803,   * * *   "   dau.of Thomas

24 Nov.1800, Kemp,   Green   Sally Broadus dau.of Shipley

24 Apr.1809, Kennedy,   Jesse   Susanna Manson

20 Mar.1808,   James J.   Mary A.Robins

 3 Nov.1830,   Joseph A.   Julia A.Parish

13 Jan.1843,   Sidney M   Mary E.Callis

7 Feb.1844, Kennedy,	Thomas H. to	Martha Pritchett dau.of Edmund
14 Dec.1791,	William	Rebecca Jordan, Bennett Goodrum sec.
3 June 1806,	"	Erman Browder
11 June 1835	" B.	Lucretia A.Parish
5 April 1786,	" H.	Betsy Pilkington, Richard Pilkington sec.
* Feb.1753, Kennon,	Joseph	Frances Ridout wid.of Giles.(OB.IV; 434)
20 June 1809,Kidd	Joseph	Sally Pennington
11 Sept.1836,	Nich.E.	Mary J.Phipps gr.dau.of Benj.
15 Oct.1837,	Richard S.	Susan S.Phipps dau.of John
26 Nov.1832,	Robert A.	Sarah A.Webb
25 July 1831, King,	Armistead	Eliz.P.Harris
31 Dec.1814,	Benjamin	Tabitha Bracey
4 Jan.1838,	" B.	Virginia Ann Bott dau.of Edward B.
30 Jan.1778,	Charles	Mary Ceely dau.of William,Merrit Ceely sec.
16 Oct.1817,	"	Ann Taylor
20 Dec.1831,	"	Mary M.Vaughan dau.of Robert
6 Nov.1843,	"	Lucy W.H.Powell
24 Aug.1783,	Edward	Winifred Ledbetter dau.of Henry
17 Dec.1787,	"	Patty Short dau.of John
26 Dec.1820,	Frederick	Patsy Gibbs
27 Apr.1820,	James	Natsy Bottom
23 Jan.1802,	John	Obedience Parham
20 Oct.1847,	" W.	Susanna Short dau.of Armistead
8 Dec.1828,	Joseph G.	Eliza Yates Gilliam born 1806.
21 Mar.1785,	Lewis	Becke Birdsong dau.of James
22 Aug.1808,	Miles	Martha Short dau.of William

64

18 Jan.1850, King,   Miles M. to Lucy Short

16 Dec.1850,   Nathaniel   Lucy Clayton

14 April 1847,   Thomas T.   Rebecca J.Doyle dau.of John

22 Dec.1794,   William   Betsy Moore, William Moore sec.

 9 Dec.1850,   "   J.   Lucy M.Bott

18 Oct.1850,   William Thos. Mary J.Moss
                            s.of Mariah
26 May 1757,   * * *   Susanna Scoggin dau.of William(W.B.III;
                                                                             217)
12 Feb.1822, Kirby,   George   Eliz.Briggs

30 Mar.1784,   Thomas   Nancy Mallory dau.of Roger.

 2 Dec.1824,   William   Minerva W.Bonner

16 Jan.1819, Kirk,   George   Agness A.Weaver dau.of William

31 Dec.1847,   "   Ann E.Lambert

27 Nov.1848,   "   Eliz.Ann Walker

18 Nov.1764,   James   Lorana Lambert dau.of Hugh

12 Dec.1820,   William   Ann Weaver dau.of William

 5 Dec.1852, Kirkland,   David B.   Amyusta S.Kelly dau.of James

 2 June 1855,   James T.   Agness E.Bennett

10 Sept.1799,   John   Brambley Edwards dau.of Jesse

28 Oct.1816,   "   Eliz.Peebles dau.of Jesse,

25 Jan.1843,   "   Eliz.Lewis

10 May 1806,   Richard   Polly Granger

25 Oct.1851,   Robert   Margaret Percival

18 May 1856,   "   Julia Lashley

25 Dec.1815,   Thomas   Ammond Duggar

 8 May 1811,   William   Ann B.Duggar

13 Nov.1854,   "   B.   Susanna Moss dau.of Meredith

22 Dec.1817, Kirkland,   Williamson   to Susan Lee

28 Nov.1825, Laffoon,   Alexander   Nancy C.Lynch

11 Jan.1803,   Daniel   Caty Russell

28 Nov.1789,   James   Jincy Samford, Matthew Lafoon sec.

26 May 1800,   "   Eliz.R.Burks

7 Dec.1846,   " M   Ann E.Winn

10 Jan.1822,   John   Eliz.Farler

7 Mar.1840,   Parks,   Emily Thomason   dau.of Banister

12 Dec.1803,   Simon   Milly Wiltshire

7 Dec.1830, Laird,   James S.   Frances Ann Hawkins dau.of Edward

5 March 1813,Lamberd, Joel   Elsey Wright

23 Nov.1842, Lambert,   Edward L.   Martha T.Lambert

11 June 1795,   Jeremiah   Sarah Cordle dau.of John & Ann

4 Sept.1792,   Lewis   Mildred Petillo, Mary ser.to age

18 June 1811,   "   Rebecca Jones

8 Feb.1848,   Luke M   Eliz.Webb dau.of Edmund B.

27 Oct.1838,   Thomas L.   Harriett M.Orgain

13 Mar.1813, Lane,   John   Sarah E.Phillips

17 July 1816,   William M.   Martha E.Hanner

22 Jan.1783, Lang,   John   Sarah Harrison exx.of Gabriel Harrison
                                            (O.B.XIII;112)

20 Apr.1780, Langton,   John   Sarah Ann Harrison wid.of Gabriel

1 Sept.1742,Lanter,   Henry   Mary Hogan dau.of William.(D.B.II;171)

23 Aug.1779, Lashley,   Benjamin   Martha Harrison, William Harrison sec.

17 Aug.1841,   " H.   Lucy J.Gibbon dau.of Thomas

23 Sept.1771,   John   Rebecca Fletcher, Owen Myrick sec.

5 May.1801, Lashley,   William to Naomi Harrison, Robert Harrison sec.

28 July 1748,   * *   Sarah Clanton (W.B.II;150)

17 May 1778,   * *   Eliz.Warren dau.of Benjamin(W.B.V;18)

10 Nov.1785,   * *   Martha Harrison dau.of William(W.B.V;161)

26 Dec.1791, Latimore, Robert   Martha Talley 21, Jesse Penn sec.

  Apr.1788,   John Jr.   Betsy Wilson, John Wilson sec.

8 Jan.1822, Lawson,   Peter   Eliz.Walker

27 Jan.1799, Lawton   * *   Sarah Ann Blick dau.of Benj.(W.B.VI;226)

25 July 1831,Lawrence, Frank   Martha Mason

25 Jan.1816,   Thomas   Delila Jones

22 May 1819, Lawson,   Booker   Eliz.Crook

16 Dec.1835, Lanier,   Abner W.   Susan E.Field

25 Nov.1771,   Benjamin   Eliz.Parker, Hincha Pettway sec.

28 Apr.1785,   "   Ann Wilkerson wid.,Ann Lanier & Wynne
                              (O.B.VIII;156) Malone wit.to contract.

27 Aug.1804,   "   Susan Hunnicutt

13 Mar.1794,   Bird   Sary Oast, John Buckley sec.

23 Aug.1794,   Burwell   Eliz.Pepper, Elisha Riddle sec.

13 Oct.1805,   "   Eliz.McKenney

26 Dec.1791,   Collier   Lucy Berryman, Jesse Berryman sec.

24 Nov.1789,   David   Frances Harwell, Charles Harrison sec.

10 Apr.1813,   "   Eliz.Rideout

25 May 1774,   Drury   Tabitha Eanes, Joseph Peebles sec.

26 Aug.1793,   Edmund   Patsey Walton, George Walton sec.

23 Jan.1797,   Frederick Tempy Warren, Herbert Hill sec.

20 Nov.1805,   Henry   Martha Owen, Robert Owen's consent

13 Nov.1816,   James   Polly Edwards

27 July 1789, Lanier,	John	to	Selah Saunders dau.of Edward decd.
15 Nov.1806,	"		Polly Wilson dau.of John
24 June 1815,	"		Martha Hawkins
25 Nov.1752,	Lewis		Martha Speed,James Speed sec.
25 Sept.1815	"		Martha Hawkins dau.of Edward
12 Dec.1787,	Nocholas		Patsy Malone dau.of George,sis.of Miles
26 Nov.1834,	Richard		Sarah Gibbs
8 Sept.1759,	Robert		* * Jackson dau.of John
24 Nov.1800,	"		Nancy Harrison
24 Sept.1752,	Sampson		Eliz.Chamberlayne dau.of Samuel(W.B.III; 84)
4 Jan.1821,	Samuel		Martha Saunders
16 Oct.1792,	Sterling		Hummons Westmoreland, Arthur Fort sec.
23 Feb.1803,	"		Polly Avery
3 July 1735,	Thomas		Ann Maclin dau.of William (Vol.1;189)
22 Aug.1794,	"		Polly Vaughan, Thomas Vaughan sec.
4 Apr.1807,	"		Mary Branch Parham
7 Nov.1809,	"		Mary Peebles
5 Nov.1810	"		Martha Dunkley
4 June 1822,	"		Mary G.Wilkes
19 Oct.1824,	" W.		Eliz.S.Bass
27 July 1772,	William		Eliz.Burch dau.of Richard Sr.
30 Apr.1821,	" H		Martha J.Pennington
17 Nov.1770,	* * *		Sarah Nance dau.of William(W.B.IV;31)
13 Nov.1772,	* * *		Mary Cook dau.of Henry (W.B.IV;241)
9 June 1779,	* * *		Caty Quarles dau.of Hubbard (W.B.V;107)
21 Sept.1803, Leach,	John		Susan Parham

22 Oct.1804,	Ledbetter,	Hamlin to	Dicey Wright
2 Dec.1742		Henry	Edith Williamson dau.of John(D.B.II;204)
16 Dec.1808		Hubard	Thirza Moseley
22 Dec.1797,		Isaac	Nancy King, William Carpenter sec.
6 Oc t.1841,		John W.	Maria Louisa Goodwyn dau.of Nancy
7 Dec.1809,		Osborne	Polly Delbridge
5 Nov.1741,		Richard	Mary Walton dau.of George & Eliz.(O.B.II; 50)
12 Nov.1838,		William O.	Sarah E.Delbridge
27 Feb.1785,		* * *	Ann Johnson dau.of John.(W.B.V;154)
27 Feb.1785		* * *	Jane Johnson dau.of John " " "
19 Dec.1801,	Lee,	David	Fanny Moore
22 Dec.1810,		James	Clerky Kelly
21 May 1792,		Jesse	* * Abernathy sister of Charles(W.B.VI; 55)
27 July 1846,	Leigh,	William L.	Eliz.L.Howell
25 Jan.1802,	Lench	Syreck	Sally Moseley
19 Aug.1844,	Lewellin,	Charles H.	Eliz.P.Barner dau.of Harrison
18 Mar.1770,		Thomas	Sarah Adams, Seymour Powell sec.
8 Sept.1787,	Lewis,	Benjamin	Eliz.Edmunds dau.of John Flood Edmunds
15 Dec.1823,		"	Jr.Harriet S.Booth
21 Dec.1831,		Frederick A	Eliz.Moss dau.of Sally
22 Feb.1836,		"	" Elmira B.Kelly
25 June 1787,		Harbert	Charlotte Betty dau.of Thos.,Grow.Owen sec.
6 Oct1832,		Hiram	Mary Kirkland
28 Feb.1820,		James	Ann Lewis dau.of William
18 Dec.1821,		"	Jincy Nunnally
25 Dec.1848,		"	Martha Wray

28 Jan.1793, Lewis,	John	to	Lucy Maclin, Thomas Maclin sec.
26 Oct.1835,	"		Sophia Sadler dau.of Henry
7 Aug.1787,	Reuel		Silvey Abernathy dau.of Frederick
4 Dec.1818	Rewell		Eliz.Medlin
10 Apr.1823,	Stephen		Judy Jones
20 Dec.1819,	William		Eliz.Scoggin
28 Oct.1844,	Willis		Rose A.Crighton
27 Sept.1763,	Zebulon		Sandal Jackson dau.of Henry(D.B.VII;432)
14 Mar.1780, Lett,	James		Lucy Hubbard, Thomas Grubbs sec.
24 Nov.1779,	John		Jean Whitfield
6 Feb.1801,	"		Eliz.Walker
24 Dec.1794,	William		Polly Duggar dau.of John
4 June 1741, Liderdale	William ?		Jean Clemons wid.of John.(O.B.II)
24 Nov.1786, Lightfoot	Claiborne		Betsy Wray dau.of John
6 Jan.1819,	Claxton		Clara Winn
14 Aug.1823,	John		Mary Penn
4 Jan.1803, Lilley	Nathaniel		Judith King
17 Apr.1800, Linch	Adin		Sally Jones
9 Mar.1813,	Aiden		Polly Dobbins
27 June 1803,	Lewis		Amey Moseley
25 Oct.1800,	William		Nancy Wright
1 Aug.1733,	* * *		Rachel Linch dau.of Francis(Vol.1;109)
22 Feb.1739,	* * *		Anne Jackson dau.of John (O.B.II;127)
10 Dec.1840, Locke,	James B.		Nancy Allen
18 Dec.1812,	Richard		Frances Dunkley
15 Dec.1809, Lockett,	Philip		Jane Trotter

5 Nov.1798, Love,	Allen to	Mary Edmunds dau.of Sterling
5 Nov.1793,	Edward	Lucy Harrison 21, Theophilus Harrison sec.
4 April 1771,	Hugh	Eliz.Huling Thomas gr.dau.of Edward
22 Mar.1798,	John	Frances Harrison, James Harrison sec.
13 Nov.1772, Lowd,	* *	Anne Cook dau.of Henry (W.B.IV;241)
4 Jan.1745, Loyd,	* *	Sarah Mattox (.O.B.II;129)
16 March 1758,	John	Eliz.Evans dau.of Eliz.
24 Dec.1753,Loyall,	Thomas	Rebecca Tatum, Peter Tatum sec.
16 Oct.1787,Loyed,	William	Lucy Scarborough dau.of William
12 Dec.1796,Loyd,	Henry	Sally Patillo, Lewis Brown sec.
1 Aug.1803,	Stephen	Eliz.Johnson
6 Nov.1746,	John	Eliz.Evans dau.of John(O.B.III;233)
19 Dec.1797,	William	Polly Thrift, Joseph Samford sec.
13 Nov.1759,Lucas,	David,	Eliz.Collier dau.of William(W.B.III;324)
1 Sept.1825,	Edmund T.	Martha Turner
24 May 1819,	James B.	Frances A.Percival
24 May.1815,	John H.	Martha Hobbs
11 Apr/1747,	Samuel	Rebecca Wyche dau.of Francis (O.B.II;148)
11 Apr.1747,	William	Eliz.Wyche dau.of Francis " " "
2 Dec.1770,	* * *	Betty Cocke (W.B.IV;151)
25 Apr.1836, Lucy,	Benjamin	Amanda E.A.Abernathy dau.of Raleigh.
9 Apr.1754,	Burwell	* * * Denton dau.of Sarah (W.B.III;142)
9 Jan.1797,	Frederick	Ann Burge dau.of Nathaniel, William Kelly sec.
18 Jan.1814,	"	Susan Kelly
20 Nov.1829,	"	Julia H.Cheely
18 Dec.1792,	Isham	Eliz.Johnson dau.of William .

27 Feb.1797, Lucy,	Jesse	to	Betsy Westmoreland
16 Feb.1825,	"		Jane House
21 Aug.1839,	John		Margaret B.Moore
18 Sept.1787,	Joshua		Eliz.Kelly, Thomas Ingram sec.
28 Feb.1820,	"		Ann L.Hunicutt dau.of Benjamin
4 Nov.1794,	Robert		Mary Kelly Browder dau.of Joseph
21 Oct.1799,	"		Catherine Abernathy
21 Nov.1824,	Samuel K.		Martha Ann Abernathy
17 Dec.1839,	" "		Martha Hardaway
20 Mar.1819	Theophilus		Tabitha Gresham
19 Dec.1837,	Thomas		Julia Ann Lanier
13 Apr.1837, Lundie,	Benjamin L.		Ariana M. King dau.of Miles
27 Jan.1817,	Green H.		Nancy Bass
26 Mar.1827,	James M.		Emily H.Brodnax
7 Dec.1842,	" B.		Sophronia Hartwell
26 Nov.1827,	John M.		Martha P.Short
5 Jan.1832,	Thomas F.		Winifred F.Cheely
20 Oct.1778,	William		Lydia Garris dau.og Hannah
11 Mar.1819, Lunsford,	Robert A.		Cetian Harris
24 Dec.1753, Lyall,	Thomas		Rebecca Tatum
5 Nov.1832 Lynch,	Benjamin,		Jane A.Clary
6 Jan.1823,	Gilbert		Susan Clegg
24 Nov.1834,	Green H.		Eliz.W.Wray
11 Jan.1822,	James C.		Nancy Pearson
17 Dec.1845,	James M.		Arian F.Fenn dau.of Mildred E.
13 Dec.1838,	Jones C.		Rebecca Smith dau.of Pleasant

22 May.1848,Lynch,   Thomas C.R. to Sarah J.Burton dau.of William G.

21 Apr.1791,McConico,   Christopher   Mary Stith, Peter Jones sec.

28 Dec.1799,McCullick,   Cad   Dolly Rideout

27 Mar.1819,McCulloch,   Edward   Eliz.Whitlock

3 Mar.1788,McDaniel,   John,   Betty Collier, Richard Stone sec.

27 Jan.1782,McInvale,   James   Jane Stainback dau.of Francis

25 Apr.1786,McInvale,   * * *   Mary Woodrough, Zacha. Sims sec.

17 Feb.1796,   * * *   Mary Stainback (W.B.VI;58)

25 Mar.1816,McKenny,   Benjamin W.   Tabitha Williams

8 Dec.1827,   Green   Lindy R.Nunnally

25 Feb.1828,   Samuel   Mary Ann Martin

17 Feb.1799,   * * *   Mary Mitchell dau.of John(W.B.VI;245)

1 Nov.1802,   * * *   Frances Wheeler dau.of Benjamin)" 513)

29 Jan.1751,McKnight,   William   Judith Maclin dau.of William (W.B.III;70)

26 Mar.1804,McRobert,   Ebenezer M.   Henrietta M.Field

15 Jan.1784,Mabry,   Gray   Martha Watson dau.of William,Ro.Watson
                                                          sec.

22 June 1747,   Hinchia   Anna Jackson,   (O.B.IV;31)

1 Jan.1752,   * *   Ann Courtney widow D.B.V;143)

28 May 1787,   Dolly Clack dau.of John deceased.& Mary

10 Sept.1770,   Joshua   * * * *,John Clack sec.

10 Sept.1770,   Jordan of Meck.Ann Hansell dau.of James

16 Feb.1773,   Lewis   Susanna Hamilton, John Hamilton sec.

19 Dec.1812,   Nathaniel   Martha M.Elliott

1 Apr.1778,   Robert s.Nath. Rebecca Stewart

16 June 1773,   Seth   Eliz.Seawell, Benjamin Seawell sec.

2 Dec.1742, Mabry,	* * * to	Sarah Williamson dau.of John,(D.B.II;204)
14 Nov.1779, Maclin,	Augustine C.	Polly Jones
14 Nov.1799,	Augustus W.	Patty Jones
8 June 1771,	James	Eliz. Maclin dau.of John
22 Jan1783,	"	Lucy Jones dau.of Ann & John Robert decd. (O.B.XIII;99)
23 Jan.1753,	John	Susan Douglas (O.B.III;107)
29 Mar.1773,	" Co.	Anne Cryèr wid. Joseph Peebles sec.
* May 1752,	"	Susanna Douglas dau.of John
17 Feb.1806,	" D.	Charlotte Edmunds
16 Dec.1833,	" F.	Ann D.Lundy
14 Mar.1791,	Joseph	Nancy Walker dau.of David
18 Oct.1832,	Lewis S.	Martha Hunwell dau.of John
14 July 1800,	Thomas	Julia Edmunds
25 Sept.1754,	William Jr.	Sally Clack dau.of James
28 June 1830,	" W.	Lucy C.Walker
4 May 1813, Madison,	James	Susanna Edmunds dau.of Thomas
23 Dec.1822, Macon,	Nathaniel	Margaret A.Barrow dau.of Arabella.
7 Oct.1828, Maddox,	John P.	Parthenia G.Hudson
25 Sept.1786,Maddux,	Lazarus,	Hannah Jones wid.of John R. decd.
8 May 1831,	Littleton	Ann Eliza Matthews
5 Dec.1832,	Samuel of Lun.	Martha F.Jones dau.of Reps.
29 Sept.1781,	Wilfred	Lucretia Bishop dau.of Mathew
11 July 1843,	William H.	Martha C.Seymore
19 Oct.1801, Madelin	* *	Sally Duggar dau.of John.(W.B.VI;189)
2 Oct.1793, Mainyard,	* *	Mary Ingram dau.of Joseph,(W.B.V;520)
23 Aug.1790, Meiss	* *	Lucy Clary dau.of Harwood,(W.B.V;381)

19 Dec.1842, Maitland,	Hiram to	Agness S.Maitland dau.of William
25 Sept.1797,	Richard	Sally Duggar, John Duggar sec.
22 April 1816,Maidland,	* *	Rhody Lewis
3 Sept.1849 Maitland	Ruel	Martha Lewis
21 Dec.1826,	Samuel	Martha Lewis
19 Dec.1842,	Wyatt	Mary Jane Maitland dau.of William
29 Sept.1849	"	Eliza Jane Wray dau.of Anderson
3 Jan.1806, Major,	Samuel	Eliz.Green dau.of Dorothy
9 Nov.1822, Mallory,	Alexander	Eliz.Short dau.of William ?
7 Apr.1818,	James B.	Cleora Maclin dau.of Augustine W.
23 Oct.1788,	Roger Jr.	Tabitha Baugh ward of Sarah
24 May 1786,	William	Sarah Atkins, Zacha.Sims sec.
8 Dec.1823,	" Y.	Eliz.P.Edwards
5 Aug.1832, Malone,	Claiborne	Eliz.Vaughan
17 Mar.1838,	*	Mary J.Smith dau.of George
27 Jan.1777,	George	Lucy Carter, James Marshall sec.
9 May 1807,	James	Martha Davis dau.of John
8 Nov.1845,	John D.	Jane C.Williams
24 Nov.1806,	" P.	Sally Hobbs dau.of Hubbard
21 Oct.1776,	Michael	Cicely Petway, Nathaniel Malone sec
28 June 1777,	* * *	Eliz.Dailey dau.of William(W.B.V;2)
7 Aug.1794,	* * *	Lucy Curtis, (W.B.VI;56)
19 Oct.1839, Mangump	James H.	Susan C.Mangum
16 Sept.1844,Manly,	Benjamin F.	Lucy Ann Stone
20 Nov.1822, Mann,	Spencer A.	Harriet J.Thompson
31 July 1820,Manning,	Caleb	Sally Manning

7 Oct.1828, Manning,	Caleb	to Rebecca Huff dau.of Lewis
23 Jan.1786,	Joßel	Mary Owen dau.of William, William Owen sec.
3 Dec.1811,	John	Eliz.L.Banks
23 June 1828,	"	Sarah W.Blanch
19 May 1846,	Lewis	Martha Stewart
27 July 1807,	Thomas	Sally Seward
24 Mar.1794,	William	Nancy Manning, Caleb Manning sec.
27 Sept.1802,	"	Eliz.Seward
24 Aug.1812,	"	Frances Betty
8 Dec.1838,	" M.	Jane C.Britt
11 Dec.1815, Manson,	Edward	Nancy W.Maclin
10 Nov.1828,	Hardaway	Ann Stradford
25 Jan.1790,	John	Eliz.Rogers dau.of John, Thomas Manson sec.
19 May 1821,	" R.	Catherine Read dau.of Thomas decd.
23 Apr.1821,	Thomas H.	Mary E.Maclin
25 May 1826,	" J.	Susan J.Maclin
30 July 1799,Marable,	Benjamin	Lucy Barner dau.of John
9 May 1818,	Henry H.	Ann E.Richardson dau.of Jordan
23 April 1846,	Thomas E.	Mary T.Morrison
9 Dec.1803, Marks,	Samuel	Martha L.Morris
10 Dec.1798,	Thomas	Martha Brown dau.of Lewis Sr.
22 June 1829,	William	Sally Baugh Wilson dau.of John
2 Oct.1770, Marriott,	William	Mary Cocke dau.of Brazure.(O.B.XI;246)
13 Oct.1813, Marshall,	Benjamin	Sally H.Duggar
22 Sept.1795,	Ichabod	Sarah Harwell, Buckner Harwell sec.
5 June 1789,	James	Mary Williams, Lew.Williams sec.

5 Aug.1799, Marshall,	John to	Patty Jones Wynne, Peter Wynne sec.
5 Aug.1799,	"	Betty Jones, Peter Wynne sec.
5 Dec.1821,	Peter	Margaret A.Short
10 Oct.1796,	Spain	Unity Johnson, Edmund Collier sec.
20 July 1829,	Stephen	Catherine Cross
10 Nov.1785,	* * *	Ann Harrison dau.of William.(W.B.V;161)
9 Oct.1825,	William	Rebecca Wall
6 Jan.1825, Martin,	Henry	Molly Lanier dau.of Eliz.
27 Aug.1830,	* *	Anna Medlin dau.of Rebecca
28 July 1834,	William	Eliz.Maitland
27 July 1840, Mateer,	Hugh	Julia Ann Rowlett
10 Nov.1806, Massenburg,	John Jr.	Sarah C.Jones
29 Jan.1825,	Thomas	Tabitha H.Powell
19 Dec.1772, Massey,	* *	Eliz.Reives dau.of George (W.B.IV;135)
17 July 1786,	* *	Frances Nanney dau.of John (W.B.V;283)
26 Dec.1810,	William	Margaret Kelly
30 Jan.1847,	"	Rhoda Kelly
27 July 1772, Mason,	Charles	Mary Burch dau.of Richard Sr.
26 Dec.1814,	George	Eliz.Maclin
25 Feb.1836,	Dr. "	Lucy B.Jones dau.of Mary A.
24 Nov.1834,	Henry N.	Martha J.Manson, dau.of Nancy
23 May1808,	James	Polly Hancock
24 July 1765,	John	Jane Thweatt exx.of William(O.B.IX;400)
9Feb.1799,	" R.	Sarah H.Cargill, John Jones sec.
4 Mar.1783,	Joseph	Eliz.Watson dau.of William, Edw.Webb sec.
15 Dec.1807,	Nathaniel,Nancy Trotter	

27 Dec.1798, Mason,   * *   to Patsy Smith dau.of Richard (W.B.VI;219)

15 Dec.1847, Matthews, Charles   Eliz.Hagood

19 Dec.1802,   Drury   Polly Wynne

24 Apr.1819,   Edmund   Polly Walker

22 Dec.1838,   Henry H.   Sarah L.Watts dau.of Lucy

10 Dec.1788,   James   Eliz.Hardie, Abraham Cocke sec.

 5 Nov.1842,   " P.   Eliz.Connell

26 May 1780,   John   Rebecca Laurence, John Laurence sec.

 3 Dec.1790,   "   Nancy Quarles dau.of Moses.

 7 Dec.1811,   "   Nancy S.Collier

14 Jan.1836,   " A.   Frances A.Boram

25 Dec.1809,   Luke   Hannah B.Jones dau.of Samuel

20 Feb.1841,   "   Harriet G.Shelton

26 Apr.1802,   Samuel   Susanna Eppes

31 Dec.1763,   William   Susanna Read dau.of William (W.B.IV;393)

26 Oct.1807,   "   Rebecca Tayler

15 Feb.1848,   Williamson Ann Eliza Parham dau.of Nicholas

26 Aug.1788,   Vines   Ann Morehead Dameron dau.of Sarah

 9 June 1779,   * *   Betsy Quarles dau.of Hubbard (W.B.V;107)

 9 June 1779,   * *   Ann Quarles dau.of Hubbard (W.B.V;107)

21 Dec.1796, Mathis,   Matthew   Eliz.Floyd dau.of Ann, Morris Floyd sec.

11 June 1792,   Sugar Jones Angelica Jones Mathis, William Elmore sec.

18 Oct.1808, May,   John Fitz:^h Margaret B.Field

19 May,1756,   Joseph   Ann Jones widow, William Bishop sec

19 Dec.1785, Mayes,   William   Rebecca Morriss, Lester Morriss sec.

14 July 1821,Mayton,   George   Rebecca Lambert

5 June 1797, Meacham,   James   to Polly Seward, John Seward sec.

5 Dec.1809,   Jesse   Polly Birchett

6 Nov.1829,   "   Mildred Hanks,

18 Sept.1772, Meade,   Andrew   Susanna Stith dau.of Buckner
            of Nansemond
17 July 1833,   John A.   Eliza J.Turnbull

14 Mar.1838,   Oliver H.   Mary E.Bonner dau.of Martha

15 Sept.1832,   Theophilus Susan Edmunds Haskins ward of R.K.Meade

23 Jan.1804, Mealer,   George   Olive Harrison dau.of Cuddy

24 July 1809,Mealey,   James   Mary Meanly (Manly?)

28 Sept.1772,   Richard   Keziah Freeman, Joshua Wingfield sec.
                                                    (D.B.XII; 109)
6 Dec.1793, Meanly,   Richard   Eliz.Traylor, Edward Traylor sec.

26 Nov.1787, Medley,   Isaac   Sarah Lester   O.B.XIV;206)

1 Mar.1801, Meeton,   Thomas Jr. Eliz.Jones

1 Sept.1742,Megran   Edward,   Obedience Hogan dau.of William(D.B.II;171

20 Jan.1782, Meredith,   David Jr.   Eliz.Wingfield dau/ of Joshua

27 Sept.1787,   "   "   Mary A.Mason

12 Dec.1846,   "   W.   Eveline G.Clarke

* * *   Meredith,   John M.   * *   *

8 Oct.1812,   Thomas H.   Jane Jordan ward of W.Grigg

11 July 1820,   William   Lucy W.Gee dau.of John

27 June 1848,   Thomas H.   Henrietta T.Trotter

24 Nov.1801,   William   Writter Hamlet

11 Dec.1824, Merrit,   Alexander   Erminia E.Love

24 Dec.1804.   Charles   Fortune Jackson

4 July 1762,   Mary Embry dau.of Henry

17 May 1767, Metcalf,   * *   Ann Sexton

3 July 1735,	Michell,	John to	Judah Maclin dau.of William (Vol.1;180)
21 Jan.1840,	Mikeal,	William	S.A.J.Kirkland
22 Dec.1800,	Miller,	Jacob.	Nancy Brown
17 Dec.1801,	Minor,	Anslem	Patsy Cook
18 Oct.1786,		Peter	Hannah Jones dau.of Peter
11 Oct.1785,		Thomas	Tabitha Williams, William Williams sec.
2 Aug.1796,	Mitchell	Abram	Rebecca Hawthorn, Peter Hawthorn sec.
28 Oct.1828,		Drury	Martha Delbridge
8 Nov.1812,		Henry P.	Sally Biggs
30 Jan.1821		" W.	Middy Mize
20 Dec.1806,		Jesse	Patsy Adkins
26 Aug.1816,		Johr	Susan Biggs dau.of Richard
13 Dec.1823,		"	Ann Pearcy dau.of Richard
10 Sept.1798,		Joshua	Prudence Phillips, Thoman Phillips con.
15 Feb.1803,		Marcus	Eliz.Parham
23 Dec.1825,		Ransom	Jane T.Collins
25 Oct.1807,		Robert	Nancy C.Buckner
13 Jan.1803,		"	Polly Collier
26 Oct.1807,		Thomas	Ann Moore
26 June 1817,		"	Sally J.Bishop dau.of John
14 Dec.1831,		Washington C.	Minerva M.Allen
13 Jan.1759,		William	Mary Spears dau.of William & Ann
23 Dec.1835,		"	Mary Ann C.Biggs
20 June 1769,		* * *	Sarah White dau.of Samuel (W.B.IV;56)
27 Nov.1774,		* * *	Eliz.Clark dau.of Joshua, (W.B.IV;244)
29 Aug.1779,		* * *	Sarah Thweatt (W.B.V;73)

24 Sept.1788,Mitchell,   * * * to Becky Birchett dau.of Jane (W.B.V;341)

27 June 1801,Mize,   Dennis,   Amey Ray

25 Dec.1820,   Holmes   Susan Wesson

 2 Jan.1794,   Henry   Keziah Overby, Cheslin Curtis sec.

24 Jan.1791,   Jeremiah   Martha Mize, Jeremiah Maze Sr.sec.

 4 Oct.1830,   Wilson   Sarah King dau.of Mariah

16 Dec.1811, Moody,   Benjamin   Eliz. Hill

25 June 1832,   "   Susan H.Duggar

 4 Oct.1773,   * * *   Ann Collier dau.of Charles(W.B.IV;247)

 5 Aug.1833, Moore,   Alfred   Rebecca J.Beasley

18 Dec.1818,   Allan   Lydia Nanny dau.of John

27 Mar.1823,   Anderson   Mary Bishop

11 Jan.1791,   Benjamin   Eliz.Laffoon, Mathew Laffoon sec.

25 Nov.1805,   "   Patsy Moody dau.of Jeney

19 Dec.1827,   "   Mary Finch dau.of Sally

22 July 1833,   David   Martha L.Harrison

24 Nov.1845,   D.W.   Eliz.Parsons

22 Aug.1791,   Edward   Caty Seward, Thomas Washington sec.

 3 Apr.1774,   James   Sally Johnson dau.of Moses

21 Feb.1800,   "   Martha Hearn

18 Oct.1810,   "   Lucy Bass

29 Mar.1760,   John   Faithy Collier dau.of Thomas (W.B.III;335

19 Dec.1825,   "   Ann P.Braswell dau.of John

23 Feb.1807,   " F.   Nancy A.Fletcher

 1 Dec.1835,   " J.   Martha Cary Green

 6 Dec.1848,   " N.   Nancy P.Woodruff

17 Dec.1835, Moore,	John R.to	Polly Edwards
21 Feb.1831,	Joseph	Mary Thomason
17 Dec.1804,	Richard	Susanna Foster dau.of Eliz.
16 Dec.1844,	Robert B.	Susan Rawlings
20 Dec.1834,	Robinson	Eliz.Buckner dau.of John
22 June 1812,	Samuel	Sarah Mize
28 Jan.788,	Sterling	Sarah Edwards, Jesse Braswell sec.
24 Jan.1803,	Thomas	Rhoda Nanny
30 Nov.1829,	Sterling W.	Tabitha Braswell
8 Jan.1798,	Thomas	Mary Thompson, Thomas Moore cer.to age
21 Nov.1849	Thomson	Martha C.W.Pennington
24 Feb.1817,	Turner	Sarah Justice
2 Dec.1789,	William	Prisey Jones
11 May 1795,	"	Frances Miskell, Jeremiah Miscell sec.
17 July 1797,	"	Franky Justice, Willie Wesson sec
20 Nov.1798,	"	Priscilla Harris
13 Dec.1800,	"	Nancy Hampton, Jeremiah Hampton sec.
18 May 1813,	"	Eliz.Dailey
28 Oct.1833,	" B.	Clary Abernathy
8 May 1770,	* * *	Martha Massey dau.of Ann,(W.BIV;28)
17 July 1786,	* * *	Sylvanus Nanney dau.of John.(W.B.V;283)
12 Dec.1788, Moreland,	Francis	Hannah Rivers dau.of Thomas
6 July 1813,Morenor,	Henry	Mary Ann Eldride
4 Sept.1832,Montgomery	John C.	Eliz.C.Mitchell
18 Feb.1848, Morgan,	Andrew	Eliz.A.Ezell dau.of Buckner D.
26 Nov.1842,	John B.	Mary S.Lambert

15 Mar.1817, Morgan	Joseph	to	Susan Cheely
3 Dec.1785,	Samuel		Sally Jones dau.of Ann, B.Stith Jr.sec.
17 Nov.1783,	Thomas		Eliz.Maclin dau.of Henry.
3 Feb.1762,	* *		Mary Samford dau.of William
24 Jan.1803, Morris,	Benjamin		Martha Clayton
10 Mar.1810,	" S.		Nancy Duggar
24 Sept.1810,	Edward		Dolly Edwards
26 Dec.1785,	Henry		Mason Simmons, Thomas Stith sec.
6 Nov.1805,	Isarel		Lucy Sturdivant
30 Mar.1777,	James		Eliz.Thompson, (W.B.V;5)
28 Nov.1836,	Jesse		Sarah J. Saunders
22 Aug.1782,	John		Eliz.Edwards dau.of Thomas
16 Dec.1784,	Lester		Francis Brown dau.of Lewis,Lewis Brown Jr.sec.
13 Nov.1821,	Richard B.		Mary McKenney dau.of Mary
9 Sept.1794,	Robert		Sally Thompson, John Christian sec.
24 July 1815,	Richard B.		Julia B.Stith
10 July 1810,	Robert		Martha Floyd
24 Dec.1832,	Sanford J.		Frances P.Saunders
18 Dec.1798,	Sherrod		Amy Floyd
* Apr.1759,	Thomas		Rebecca Morris dau.of William(O.B.VII; 337)
11 Feb.1847,	"		Eliza A.Bacon
1 Nov.1802,	* *		Lucy Wheeler dau.of Benj.W.B.VI;513}
11 Mar.1772, Moss,	* *		Catherine Price dau.of John(W.B.IV;88)
22 Feb.1825, Morrison,	Edward A.		Mary C.Turnbull
* Jan.1848,	Robert J.		Harriet R.Hackley
9 Sept.1807,Moseley,	Cuddy		Nelly Mosely, William Harrison sec.

24 Aug.1821, Moseley, Nichodemus to Tabitha Mosely

 1 Sept.1818,   Samuel   Eliz.A.White

 2 Jan.1797,   Stephen   Nancy Gunn dau.of William, Peter Read
                                                                                      sec.
24 Nov.1788,   Thomas   Tabitha Bithshurs dau.of Thomas

 8 Apr.1760   * *   Eliz.Beck dau.of Andrew

13 June   * *   Martha Steed dau.of John(W.B.V;282)

 3 May 1796   * *   Winney Read dau.of James (W.B.VI;66)

 * * 1820, Moss,   David   Nancy House

27 Dec.1819,   Isaac   Jinty Santy dau.of Aggy.

 7 Sept.1807,   Marcellus   Olive Huff

 8 Aug.1821,   Nathaniel   Lucretia Hicks dau.of Fanny

28 Oct.1799,   Wilkins   Anna Jackson

 6 May 1798,   Sampson   Ann Allgood 21, Lewis Saunders sec.

28 Sept.1756,Murphey,   William   Lucy Hickman, George Summers sec.

12 June 1797,Murrell,   John   Rebecca Hardaway

25 Nov.1778, Myrick,   * *   Sarah Ledbetter dau.of Mary.

26 July 1790,Naney,   Shade   Mary Wright dau.of John.

 5 Jan.1810, Nanney   Abel   Mary Justice

25 Dec.1819,   Claiborne   Patsy Marshall

26 Nov.1810,   Daniel   Patsy Taylor

23 Dec.1836,   Drudy D.   Eliz.Smith dau.of Pleasant

 3 Dec.1800,   Jordan   Oney Gregory

17 Mar.1802, Napper,   * *   Nancy Griffiths dau.of John

31 Dec.1832 Nash,   David   Amanda Malone

23 Nov.1840   James W.   Eliz.W.Hill

 4 Sept.1774, Nash,   * *   to Mary Wilson dau.of Henry

24 Feb.1794, Neal,   Cuthbert   Nancy Powell, Thomas Powell sec.& gdn.

 5 Aug.1769,   John   Susanna Smith dau.of Cuthbert

24 Dec.1798,   "   Milly D.House

 3 Jan.1816,   Thomas   Ann Woolsey

 2 Dec.1805, Neblett,   Edward,Capt. Ann H.Roberts dau.of Samuel

 8 May 1792, Newman,   Abner   Dorothy Stegall, Thomas Stegall sec.

22 Jan.1798, Newson,   Barham   Eliz.Howard

12 Dec.1806,   Brunham   Catherine Penn

12 Nov.1789   Thomas   Mary Jones

26 May 1796,   * *   Sarah Mason dau.of Sarah W.B.VI;57)

 1 Mar.1819, Newton   Haley   Jane Taylor

 * * 1824,   Henry   * * * *

18 Dec.1848,   John   Mary T.Drake dau.of John D.

 1 May 1773 ?Nichols,   * *   Sarah Fletcher dau.of James.(Vol.1;74)

 7 Aug.1847,   James N.   Ann E.W.Wynn

11 Feb.1796, Nicholson, John   * * Swanson dau.of Joice(W.B.VI;189)

27 Dec.1817,   " S.   Martha F.Jett

25 Nov.1828,   "   Lucinda Thrower dau.of Christopher

27 Jan.1840,   Thomas J.   Emeline S.Chapman

 7 Dec.1795, Nipper,   Allan   Nancy Griffith 21, Thomas Griffith sec.

28 June 1757,Niverson, John   Ann Tazewell infant. Arch.d Wager sec.

30 Jan.1810, Nobles,   Alexander   Rebecca Clayton

 3 Oct.1843,   Mansfield   Mary W.Poyner dau.of Diggs

 4 Nov.1789,   * * *   Eliz.Harris dau.of Math.(W.B.V;344)

28 Dec.1840, Nolley,   Augustus   Margaret J.Manning

13 Jan.1798, Nolley,	James to	Martha Seward, John Seward sec.
17 Aug.1793,	John	Nancy Dance of age, Nath.Lucas sec.
24 Dec.1832,	" A.	Wilmouth Clark
8 Feb.1841, Nolly	Needham W.	Nancy R.Browder
20 Mar.1804,	Neremiah	Sally Wynne
24 May.1802,	Neverson	Fanny Seward
4 Dec.1801,	Richard	Nancy Marks
24 Jan.1804	Thomas	Mary Sadler,
13 July 1805,	"	Rebecca Rogers
15 Oct.1829,	" M.	Mary Laffoon
1 Jan.1774,	* * *	Lucy Mitchell dau.of Thomas
24 Oct.1825, Northington,	Samuel	Eliza Caroline Stith dau.of Henry
27 Nov.1774, Nott,	* * *	Amey Clark dau.of Joshua (W.B.IV;244)
28 Dec.1789, Norward	John	Sarah Norris, Thomas Norris sec.
22 May 1786, Ogborn,	Benjamin	Martha Davis, William Ogborn sec.
26 Mar.1787,	"	Sally Cook, Robert Morris sec.
25 Jan.1785, Ogburn,	Hartwell	Catherine Browder dau.of Urias
24 Mar.1809,	Henry W.	Lucy Perry
7 Nov.1815,	Sterling	Nancy Pritchett
25 Feb.1771,	William	Hannah Warren, Benjamin Warren sec.
11 Dec.1849,	"	Martha A.Williams
4 Feb.1799, Oldham	Bishop	Eliz.Hampton
16 Nov.1796,	Charles	Patsy Wynne dau.of Peter
4 Jan.1814,	"	Martha Bishop
13 Oct.1813,	Edward T.	Martha Sims dau.of Howell

29 Dec.1786, Oaldham,	Isaac	to Winifred Tarpley, Charles Tarpley sec
23 Dec.1799,	Richard	Eliz.Mares
13 Jab.1802,	"	Tabitha Rives
20 Sept.1766,Oliver,	John	Fanny Cocke dau.of Brazure,(W.B.IV;32)
24 Nov.1834, Orgain,	Benjamin	Lucy F.Manson, dau.of Nancy
10 Dec.1802,	John	Polly Birchett
30 Nov.1834,	" Dr.	Rebecca L.Orgain
4 Aug.1843,	" A,	Susan J.Trotter
18 May 1802,	Littleberry	Polly G.Johnson
30 Nov.1829,	Samuel	Jane T.Powell dau.of William H.
23 June 1803,	William	Sally Meredith
28 Nov.1792, Osborn,	"	Ann Thornton dau.of William (O.B.XVI;28)
28 Nov.1810, Oslin,	James	Mary Ann Coley
25 Nov.1799, Osmore,	Richard,	Susanna Wade
17 Mar.1813, Overby,	John	Charlotte Beard
26 Aug.1805,	Thomas	Martha Sykes
14 Dec.1815,	"	Eliz.Lucy dau.of Joshua
18 Mar.1833,	William	Martha A.E.Stith dau.of Obediah
5 Dec.1791, Owen,	Abner	Frances Davenport, John Owen sec.
2 July 1805,	Bolling	Betsy Wesson
26 Dec.1842,	Edmond	Lucreaty Moss aged 35 years.
6 Sept.1836,	Godfrey	Martha Lewis
30 Oct.1832,	Harrison	Fanny H.Dromgoole
26 June 1786,	James	Ann Wilkes dau.of Jo. decd.
1 Dec.1817	"	Martha N.Powell
22 Oct.1788,	John	Mary Stainback dau.of Littleberry decd.

20 Dec.1801, Owen,	John to	Nancy Williams
12 Oct.1833,	"	Eliz. Ezell
20 Oct.1789,	RichardB.	Susanna Edwards dau.of Capt.William
		Geronow Owen sec.
22 Dec.1778,	Robert	Sarah Richardson dau.of William
23 Nov.1795,	"	Mary Mathis, Arthur Fort sec.
15 Oct.1803,	"	Polly Lanier
7 June 1817,	"	Nelly Matthews
28 Feb.1803,	Sterling	Lurana Brewer
25 Dec.1804,	Thomas	Polly Lane dau.of Micajah
22 Dec.1806,	William	Lucy Wright
27 Nov.1815,	" R.	Polly Betty
7 Nov.1793,	* * *	* * * Simmons dau.of Susanna(W.B.V;521)
25 Aug.1794, Ozbrook,	* * *	Mary Strange dau.of Owen (W.B.V;559)
26 Nov.1769, Pace,	John	Ann Russell, John Russell sec
20 Dec.1805, Palmer,	Edward	Sally Jones
18 Oct.1844,	Luke J.	Sarah E.Grigg
22 May 1820,	Stephen	Juliet Hartwell dau.of Armi
24 Nov.1806,	William	Catherine Maclin dau.of Joseph
26 June 1843,Parham,	Edward H.M.	Tabitha A.Barnes
28 Apr.1770,	Epharim	Ann Collier dau.of Thomas,
23 Nov.1778,	"	Parthenia Gee dau.of William
19 Apr.1794,	"	Frances Harrison ward of Robert B.Owen
22 Oct.1778,	James	* * * *, Nicholas Edmunds sec.
25 Nov.1755,	Mathew	Rebecca Maclin dau.of John
22 July 1777,	Thomas	Eliz.Gilliam, William Mason sec.

20 June 1771, Parham,   William   to   Hannah Hill widow, Francis Young sec.

21 Dec.1767,   * * *   Polly Williams dau.of Jane(W.B.IV;65)

28 Jan.1794,   * * *   Eliz.Ingram dau.of Benjamib(W.B.V;575)

20 Dec.1842, Parish,   Enos W.   Eliza M.Pritchett dau.of William

8 Mar.1827,   Goodwyn   Martha Williams

1 Feb.1806,   Henry   Polly Whett

7 Jan.1796,   Jones   Vicey Rawlings, Henry Rawlings sec.

14 Jan.1840,   Lazarus   Margaret W.W.Wilkes dau.of Richard

11 Oct.1795,   Mathew   Margaret Lawler 22 yrs.,Robert Duncan
                                                                         sec.

26 Oct.1841,   "   Mary Daniel

20 Dec.1820,   Peter   Sally Dean

27 May 1797,   Thomas   * * * Edwards dau.of John (W.B.VI;147)

28 Jan.1798,   William   Jean Kennedy, Robert Kennedy sec.

3 Dec.1810,   "   Susanna Dean

5 Aug.1844, Parker,   Thomas W.   Rebecca A.B.Poole

16 Mar.1836, Parks   William W.   Ann W.Tudor

25 Aug.1806, Patterson, King   Polly Rawlings

30 Mar.1814,   Robert   Silvey Vaughan

31 Jan.1835, Patillo,   ChristopherC. Lucy Tilman dau.of Sally

24 Nov.1832,   Robert H.   Julia E.Pritchett

22 Feb.1790 Paup,   John   Sarah S.Walker, Thomas Stith Sr.sec.

6 June 1831,   " W.   Charlotte P.Maclin dau.of Joseph

18 Jan.1820,   " "   Tabitha Maclin dau.of Joseph

1 Oct.1822, Payne,   Littleton   Minerva Rideout

14 Jan.1748,   * * *   Amey Vaughan dau.of Richard (W.B.II;165)

26 May 1834, Peace,   Samuel M.   Mary A.E.Jones dau.of Robert B.

26 Dec.1835, Peace,   Willis H.to Mary F.A.Barrow dau.of John

20 June 1812,Pearcy,   Jane Slate

27 Sept.1825,Pearin,   Howell   Tilly Mitchell

17 Mar.1816, Pearson,   Drury   Nancy E.Smith

20 Nov.1843,   E.A.   Arian S.Moss

6 Jan.1840,   Gilliam   Adelaide W.Phipps gr.dau.of Benjamin

23 July 1781,   James   Susanna Day dau.of Olive

22 Feb.1792,   "   Mary Walton widow, George Walton sec.

28 Feb.1825,   Jesse A.   Mary E.Harrison dau.of Joseph

27 Oct.1794,   John   Martha Britt, Henry Britt sec.

27 Sept.1802,   "   Rebecca Wright

17 Mar.1824,   " Jr.   Middy Warmock

18 Dec.1802,   Johnson   Sally Brewer

11 July 1823,   Littleberry Edith A.B.Watson widow

28 Nov.1842,   Littleberry,Mary J.Delbridge

5 March 1800,   Littleton Sally Brewer, Benjamin Ezell sec.

22 Dec.1788,   Morris   Nancy Brewer, John Brewer sec.

8 Nov.1825,   Sterling C. Eliz.B.Pearson

5 Feb.1833,   Washington Eliz.Delbridge

23 Aug.1790,   William   * * Clary dau.of Harwood (W.B.V;381)

* Aug.1785, Pegram,   Daniel   Nancy Hardaway

24 June 1799,   Edward   Rebecca Harper,ward of Richard Coleman

7 Sept.1821,   William B. Sarah E.Walker

9 Dec.1823, Pelham,   John B.   Eliza W.Jackson

11 Apr.1791, Penick,   Nathan   Eliz.Fowlkes dau.of Thomas

18 Dec.1786, Penn,   Jesse   Charlotte Ingram, Bartho. Ingram

90

Date	Name	Spouse/Details
30 Nov.1786, Penn,	John	to Mary Briggs, Reuben Wright sec.
26 Nov.1804,	Paschal	Sally Orgean
5 Dec.1804,	Thomas	Tabitha Lucas dau.of Frederick
13 Oct.1759, Pennington,	Benjamin	* * * Bailey (W.B.III;307)
22 Dec.1795,	* * *	Patsey Floyd dau.of Charles (W.B.VI;82)
1 Dec.1841,	George W.	Martha C.W.Kirkland
21 Oct.1816,	John S.	Martha J.Wilkes
10 May 1802,	" Thos.	Betsy Pennington
30 Junr 1795,	Thomas	Mary Clarke, Benajah Saxton sec.
27 July 1799,	William	Nancy Murrell
30 Junr 1795,	" Thomas	Mary Clark
8 Aug.1814,	"	Eliz.Betty
22 Nov.1841,	" T.	Mary Jane Gee
24 Feb.1787, Penticost,	James	Lucy Saunders, Ebbin Saunders sec.
15 Oct.1810,	William	Dorothy Coleman dau.of Richard
4 Feb.1741, Pepper,	Richard	Martha Alexander wid.of John (O.B.II;85)
14 Sept.1786,	"	Subina Conneley dau.of Sarah,Lewis Connely sec.
28 Nov.1796,	William B.	Polly Williams, George Williams sec.
12 June 1736,Peebles,	* * *	Eliz.Clark dau.of Samuel (Vol.1;305)
19 Dec.1772,	* * *	Ann Reives dau.of George
8 Jan.1800,	Allen G.	Polly Smith dau.of Stephen
9 Dec.1807,	" "	Eliz.Stainback
23 Apr.1785,	Brittain	Jane Green dau.of Frederick(W.B.V;187)
13 Nov.1772,	David	Betty Cook dau.of Henry (W.B.IV;241)
23 Dec.1779,	Drury	Lucy Wilburn, John Peebles Jr/sec.
23 Mar.1784,	"	Lucy Saunders dau.of Edward.(O.B.XIII;360)

Date	Surname	Groom	Bride
4 Jan.1817,	Peebles,	Dudley to	Lucy S.Brantley
25 Dec.1832,		"	Lucy Y.Atkinson dau.of John
12 Dec.1827,		" B.	Nancy W.Baugh
28 July 1834,		Fred'k A.	Eliz.B.Baugh dau.of Litt. Baugh
22 Sept.1806,		Jesse	Eliz.Lanier
23 Apr.1810,		"	Martha Williams
11 July 1815,		"	Eliz.Smith
21 May 1819,		John B.	Sarah E.W^{y} Fletcher dau.of John
28 Nov.1758,		Joseph	Mary Robinson, Arch^{d} Wager sec.
23 Dec.1778,		Lewis,	Jean Hicks, Robert Hicks sec,
* Dec.1810,		Man	Eliz.Stainback
4 Sept.1804,		William	Eliz.Potts
11 Sept.1799,	Percivall,	Joseph	Peggy Love
25 Apr.1831,	Perkins,	David W.	Matthew J.Bishop
23 Mar.1807,		Gideon	Eliz.Jessee
12 Mar.1828,		"	Mary Short aged 40 years
27 Feb.1818,		Joel	Lucy Jackson dau.of Epharim
22 Jan.1828,		Thomas	Mary Howell dau.of S.
19 Dec.1833,		" D.	Sarah A.Driscoll
22 Dec.1800,		Young D.	Lavinia Lucy dau.of Rachel
6 Sept.1790.	Perkinson,	Archibald	Amy Harwell 21 years.Isham Perkinson sec.
17 Feb.1836,		Hezekiah	Martha K.Parish
21 Nov.1836,		John M.	Lucy C.Hawkins dau.of Uriah
9 July 1798,		Seth	Kezia Curtis, Robert Hardaway sec.
22 June 1814,		"	Polly Moss
20 Jan.1778,	Perry,	Julius	Lucy Charles

24 Oct.1833, Person,	Richard J to	Mary L.Pritchett
28 Mar.1751, Peterson,	Batte,	Frances Ranson wid.of Richard.(O.B.IV;39)
20 Dec.1805,	Jesse	Hannah Vaughan
6 Sept.1836,	William J.	Ann Hamblett
24 Mar.1800, Petillo,	John	Patsy Steed dau.of Mark
21 Dec.1790,	* *	Eliz.Floyd dau.of Josiah (W.B.V;396)
11 June 1795,	Labon	Betsey Reece, Isham Reese sec
27 Apr.1803,	"	Caty Stone dau.of Margaret
20 Oct.1809,	"	Mary Smith
2 Feb.1798,	Littleton	Judith Barnner, John Barner sec.
29 Apr.1801, Petway,	* * *	Martha Jones(Hickory Run)(sis.of George) (W.B.VI;334)
28 Nov.1786, Phenix,	Frederick	Patty Overby, Joel Biggs sec.
12 Aug.1808, "	"	Eliz.Pheonix
17 Dec.1822, Phillips,	Banjamin M.	Mary Walton
25 Nov.1823,	George S.	Mary M.Stith dau.of Ariana
3 Dec.1792,	Sterling	Mary Williams , Henry Wesson sec.
5 Nov.1787,	Thomas	Ann Clack sau.of John, Robt.Brister sec.
6 Feb.1796,	William	Nancy James, Cary James sec.
25 Mar.1746,	* * *	Celia Deloach dau.of William,(O.B.II;140)
16 Jan.1773, Phipps,	* * *	Sarah Williams dau.of Williams(W.B.IV; 473)
16 Feb.1791,	Benjamin	Lucy Turbeyfield,David Kirkland sec.
14 Dec.1831,	James N.	Mary E.Steed dau.of Jeauthan
28 Feb.1814,	John	Susan S.Neal
13 Feb.1821,	"	Nancy Harrison widow
2 Jan.1821,	William	Temperance Saxon
27 Oct.1828,	Wingfield	Eliza M.Powell dau.of Sarah

28 Sept.1837,	Phipps,	Wingfield	to	Julia Ann King
26 May 1757,	Platt,	* * *		Letitia Scoggin dau.of William(W.B.III; 217)
26 Oct.1833,	Plunkett,	John D.		Almira L.Morse
10 July 1811,	Poindexter,	Henry P.		Sally P.Paup, George Kimbrough sec.
11 Mar.1839,	Porch,	Peter		Eliz.B.Allen dau.of William
24 Dec.1824,		Thomas		Polly Wrenn dau.of Henry
22 Dec.1828,		William M.		Eliza Morse
18 Sept.1792,	Porter,	Joseph		Penelope Gee dau.of William
29 Jan.1790,		Samuel		Hannah Gee, William Gee sec.
24 Nov.1783,	Potts,	John		Susanna Daniel widow of Thomas(O.B.XIII; 294)
10 May 1797,		Solomon		Eliz.Daniel 21 years, Nathan Potts sec.
3 Dec.1786,		George		Ann Daniel dau.of Ann sr.,Jesse Potts "
5 Mar.1789,		Nathan		Betsey Dixon, Samuel Stegall sec.
7 Nov.1752,		* *		Agness Peebles wid.of Henry of Pr.Geo.
3 Mar.1795,		* *		Ann Pritchett dau.of William
12 Mar.1798,	Powell,	Edward,		Eliz.Tilman, John Harrison sec.
22 Dec.1788,		James		Nancy Gholson, William Stainback sec.
22 Apr.1861,		"		Sally Lashley
9 Apr.1799,		John		Sally Powell
24 Dec.1754,		"		Sarah Parish widow, Lucas Powell sec.
17 Dec.1832,		" L.		Susan G.Orgain dau.of Thomas
7 Dec.1829,		Marcus D.		Eliz.S.Orgain dau.of William
9 Dec.1823,		Richard D.		Eliza D.Harris
7 June 1825,		" "		Jane G.Orgain
14 Mar.1831,		Robert S.		Martha A.Powell dau.of Sarah
25 Sept.1751,		Seymour		Frances Peterson wid.⌊of Batte

22 Jan.1785, Powell,   Seymour   to   Betty Dunn dau.of William (O.B.XIII;103)

22 Jan.1800,   "   Polly Powell 21 years

25 July 1831,   William   Harriet Edmunds

12 Feb.1838,   "   C.   Adelaide H.E.Claiborne dau.of D.J.

29 Sept.1788,Power   * * *   * * * Brodnax dau.of Ann ⌊& William⌋

14 Feb.1797,   Henry   Polly Harrison 21, James Harrison sec.

24 Nov.1823,   William B.   Araminta Harrison dau.of James H.

19 Sept.1843, Poyner   David T.   Sarah A.W.James

16 Dec.1848,   "   "   Julia Reives

28 Sept.1826,   Diggs,Capt.   Eliza Purdy

 6 Dec.1837,   Henry W.   Frances E.Kirkland

29 Jan.1828, Poythress, James   Catherine S.Preston

15 Dec.1821,   Willis   Polly Brown

 1 Jan.1817, Preston,   James   Rebecca Suggett

24 Aug.1789, Price,   John   Sucky Proctor, Daniel Duggar sec.

22 Nov.1784,   Joseph,   Luvany Duggar, John Duggar Jr.sec.

15 Sept.1819,   Randolph   Eliz.Smith

28 July 1789,   Richard,   Obedience Edwards, Daniel Duggar sec.

28 Dec.1805,   Thomas D.   Edmunds

22 Apr.1800, Pride,   Thomas   Lucy Scott

18 Oct.1779, Prince,   Joel   Mourning Avent dau.of William

20 June 1826,   John J.   Martha T.Powell dau.of William H.

24 Sept.1789,   "   Eliz.Freeman dau.of Jesse.

28 Jan.1803,   * *   Ann Moseley dau.of William(W.B.VI;515)

10 Oct.1815, Pritchett,Anthony   Mary Jones

18 Aug.1814,   Asa J.   Lucrecy Brigs

27 Oct.1802, Quarles,   James   to Mary Ann Brown

14 Aug.1804,   John   Martha Burge

23 Mar.1778,   Moses   Constance Fisher, James Fisher sec.

11 Oct.1796,   William   Sally Dance, William Elmore sec.

31 Dec.1763,   * * *   Catherine Read dau.of William & Eliz.
                                                              W.B.IV;393)

13 Jan.1802, Rachel,   Francis   Sylvia Barnes dau.of William

16 Dec.1822,   James V.   Martha Vaughan

 1 Nov.1822, Ragsdale   Herbert A. Eliz.Abernathy

22 Jan.1811,   Peter   Martha Williams

23 Feb.1784,   William   Ann Scarborough dau.of Edward decd.

28 Jan.1788 Raines,   Christopher,Amy Baird dau.of John, W.Mitchell sec.

24 Apr.1780,   Hartwell   Rebecca Lucas, John Lucas sec.

17 May 1796,   Nathaniel   Susan Parham, ward of James Burks

18 May 1796,   "   Sarah Parham, John Wyche sec.

 6 Feb.1809, Rainey,   Benjamin L.,Eliz.Short

12 Sept.1821,   David   Jane Wesson

29 May 1800,   Francis   Nancy Wilson dau.of John

28 Feb.1820,   Herbert A. Clary H.Lee, John Lee sec.

30 July 1794,   Isham   Sally Firth dau.of Sarah, Wm.Firth sec.

29 Nov.1799,   James   Susanna Kirkland

16 Apr.1799,   Jessee   Frances Duggar

 2 Mar.1809,   John   Permely Edwards dau.of John

31 Mar.1797,   Nathaniel   Catherine House

15 Jan.1792,   William   Rebecca White, Blumer White sec.

26 Oct.1795,   Zebulon   Nancy Loyd dau.of John, Henry Loyd sec.

27 Nov.1826,	Pritchett,	Asa J. to	Martha T.Thweatt
26 Nov.1798,		Caleb	Sally Howerton
3 Dec.1799,		Edward	Rebecca Westmoreland, Robert W.cer.to age
30 May 1836,		"	Susan Wilkes dau.of Richard
29 Dec.1842,		" J.	Joanna H.Pritchett
9 Feb.1805,		Edwin	Polly Elmore
27 Apr.1825,		"	Jane Daniel
22 Feb.1802,		Jesse	Ruth Westmoreland
5 Dec.1820,		John	Elinor B.Daniel
29 July 1799,		Joseph J.	Winifred Williams
21 June 1824,		" S.	Eliz.A.Daniel
25 Apr.1809		Moses	Martha Ceely
23 Mar.1829,		Nicholas W.	Martha Moore
25 Sept.1826,		Richard F.	Sally Ann Edmunds dau.of Thomas
25 Dec.1805,		William	Susan Davis
21 Aug.1790,		"	Susanna Bagwell dau.of Richard(W.B.V;393)
20 Mar.1788	Proctor,	Joshua	Charity Edwards wid.,Daniel Duggar sec.
12 May 1774,		* *	Sarah Andrews dau.of Joseph
2 Aug.1808,	Pryor,	Luke,	Nancy Lane
5 July 1802,		Philip	Susan C.Wilkes
27 Oct.1789,	Pucey,	Richard	Eliz.Grubbs, Richard Biggs sec.
14 Nov.1837,	Pulliam,	John J.	Margaret Oliver
25 Dec.1800,	Purkins,	Young D.	Levinia Lucy
9 Feb.1807,	Quarles,	Benjamin	Nancy Cattles,John Quarles sec.
27 July 1785,		Croxton	Eliz.Piercy, Peter Wynne sec.

14 July 1798, Ramsey,   James   to Polly Porter dau.of John,

30 Nov.1816,   Newit,   Eliz.Tarpley

26 Sept.1778, Randle,   John   Tabitha Lyons

26 Oct.1778,   Peter   Mary Sims exx.of John(O.B.XIII;225)

 6 Mar.1738, Ranson,   Richard Frances Hicks dau.of ^Capt.Robert(W.B.II;
                                             5)

25 Jan.1811, Rash,   Joseph, Phebe Rhodes

 * * 1818,   "   Polly Ogburn

22 Sept.1797,   William Eliz.Brown

25 Sept.1777, Rawlings,   * * *   Sarah Edwards dau.of Charles(W.B.IV;521)

 5 June 1794,   * * *   Betsy Firth dau.of Thomas(W.B.V;545)

 5 Dec.1810,   Alex.   Sally Taylor

17 Jan.1799,   Benjamin Miner Wilkes 21 years.

21 Mar.1786,   Charles Sarah Allen dau.of John, Francis Mallory
                                               sec.

13 Feb.1809,   Daniel   Clarissa Ann Barnes

 7 Sept.1832,   Epha.J. Sarah Ann Winfield ward of Martha

21 Feb.1837,   George B. Nancy F.Howell dau.of Spencer

27 Mar.1820,   Hartwell Julia G.Wilkes

24 Jan.1785,   Henry   Sarah Duggar, Thomas Stith sec.

18 Feb.1817,   "   Priscilla M.Moody

25 Apr.1804,   James   Eliz.Jackson

 6 Feb.1837,   " W. Martha A.G.Harris

 8 July 1822,   John B. Nancy Meredith

19 Dec.1848,   " R.   Susan E.Kelly dau.of Samuel

10 May.1848,   Leroy T. Emily J.Hubbard dau.of Ann

10 Oct.1803,   Littleberry, Fanny Duggar

28 Jan.1839,   Nicholas Martha A.Rawlings dau.of Benjamin

| 31 Jan.1815, Rawlings, | Peterson | to | Rebecca Jackson |

31 Jan.1815, Rawlings,   Peterson   to   Rebecca Jackson

26 Jan.1789,   Randle   Eliz.Firth dau.of Thomas,John Williams
                           sec.

13 Dec.1827,   Robert   Mary D.Peebles

19 Nov.1832,   William   Nancy Harris dau.of Mary Westmoreland

15 Nov.1845,   " P.   Antoinette C.Heartwell

1 Dec.1804, Ray,   Claxton   Sally Ray

31 Oct.1805,   Francis   Vyny Linch

26 Mar.1787,   Frederick   Nancy Harwell dau.of Mary, Reuben Ray
                           sec.

27 Nov.1820,   Hicks   Nelly Wright dau.of Eliz.

18 Dec.1801, Read,   Claxton,   Amey Huskey

17 Mar.1789,   Clement   Clarissa Edmunds dau.of Thomas

2 Jan.1810,   Jesse   Susan Lundy widow

30 May 1836,   Morton   Eliz.Walker

23 Dec.1799,   Robert   Polly Brown

24 Nov.1782,   William   Susanna Grubbs

3 Feb .1762,   * *   Ann Samford dau.of William(W.B.IV;317)

20 Feb.1787, Reade   Thomas   Nancy Quarles dau.of James, John Read
                           sec.

21 Nov.1785,   William   Susanna Grubbs dau.of Hensley decd.

29 Dec.1789, Reas,   * * *   Hannah Harrison dau.of Benjamin Sr.(W.B.
                           V;345)

19 July 1808,Reaves,   Lewis,   Sally Wyche

25 Oct.1784,   Isaac   Hannah Wallace dau.of John

14 Mar.1837, Reed,   Benj.F.   Sarah A.Frisbie

2 Jan.1810,   Jessee   Susan Lundie

10 Nov.1824,   Samuel W.   Martha Pearson dau.of William

12 Dec.1843, Reeks,   Philip   Ann E.Rives

11 June 1795, Reese,	Isham to	Ann Cordle, John & Nacy Cordle permit
29 May.1800,	Joseph	Martha McCaw
29 Oct.1810,	Robert	Lucy M.Weaver
15 Oct.1816, Reid,	James G.	Harriet Starback
10 Feb.1826,	Thomas C.	Sarah Burge dau.of Martha
21 Oct.1780, Reives,	Benjamin Jr.	Dolly Haley dau.of James
* May 1791,	"	Bathin Rosser, John Rosser sec.
20 Mar.1777,	John (?)	Nancy Stewart (W.B.V;509)
7 Nov.1769,	Robert	Milly Williamson exx.of Exum(O.B.XI;216)
13 Nov.1772,	* *	Sarah Cooke dau.of Henry
9 May 1744,	* *	Hannah Donaldson dau.of Benjamin C.(W.B.IV;418)
1 Oc t.1763,	* *	Mary Jordan dau.of Thomas (W.B.IV;77)
3 May 1796,	* *	Jemima Read dau.of James (W.B.VI;66)
29 Dec.1772,	Timothy	Priscilla Turner, Robert Reives sec.
6 Apr.1738, Reynolds,	William	Joyce Sullivant wid.of Michael(O.B.1;190)
31 Mar.1787, Rice,	* *	Mary Rawlings dau.of William
7 Nov.1796,	James	Lucy West, Lewis Holloway sec.
25 Jan.1812,	Thomas	Rebecca Chambliss
4 Dec.1840, Richardson,	Amos	Mary A.M.Dunkley dau.of Z.Dunkley
18 Dec.1785,	Arthur	Eliz.Wright 21 years, John Wright sec.
12 Dec.1821,	James	Nancy Nanny dau.of Drury
14 Dec.1798,	Jordan	Susanna Duggar
12 Oct.1818,	Stith	Evalina Hartwell dau.of Armistead
23 Apr.1810,	Thomas	Eliz.Eaves
1 May 1786,	William	Ann Green widow, Lewis Brown sec.
6 Feb.1793,	"	Eliz.Yeargin, Peter Read sec.

19 Aug.1760, Richardson,	* * * to	Agness Massie dau.of Joseph(W.B.III;370)
3 May 1796,	* * *	Eliz.Read dau.of James
30 Oct.1832, Riddick,	Joseph,	Martha A.Lashley
8 June 1816,Rideout,	David,	Olive D.Saunders dau.of Jesse & Huldah
24 Nov.1793,	Jiles	Eliz.Fort ward of Isham Smith.
15 Mar.1800,	John	Mary Lanier, Charles Harrison sec
2 Jan.1787,	Jos.King	Vicky Barnes, John Rideout sec.
26 Apr.1849,	Robert A.B.	Sarah Childress dau.of Martha
11 Dec.1822,	Thomas	Eliz.A.Butts
19 Oct.1796,	William	Sarah Harwell, James Harwell sec.
15 Apr.1801, Riddle,	* *	Susanna Pepper dau.of Nathan
25 Sept.1758,Ridley,	James Day,	Mary Edwards dau.of Col.Nathaniel
1 July 1822,Rivers,	Frederick	Aggy Santy
24 July 1826,	Robert	Nanny Mason
29 May 1791,	Timothy	Priscilla Turner
2 Dec.1801,	William	Eliz.Brown
27 Jan.1799,	* *	* * Blick dau.of Benjamin(W.B.VI;226)
25 Mar.1794,	* *	Jenny Harrison dau.of Nathaniel(W.B.VI; 64)
18 May 1811, Rives	John G.	Mary B.Keatts
29 Sept.1783,	Thomas	Susanna Gee dau.of William, John Gee sec.
* * 1814,	" E.	Aphalia K.U.Tucker
28 Jan.1799, Roberd,	Abram	Betsy Thompson
24 Oct.1822, Roberts,	Caleb	Eliz.Winn dau.of Cityniah
21 Feb.1826,	Johnson	Rebecca Woodruff
13 Feb.1799,	Stephen	Amey Nanny
5 Nov.1773,	* *	Mary Pincham dau.of Samuel (W.B.IV;489)

21 Aug.1790, Roberts	William	to	Frances Bagwell dau.of Richard (W.B.V;393
21 Dec.1825,	"		Harriet Cashon dau.of Samuel
22 Apr.1833, Robertson,	Daniel H.		Mary A.C.Buford
25 Aug.1756,	Edward,		Ann Cauze widow, James Parham sec.
* Jan.1757,	"		Ann Kemp wid.of Thomas (O.B.VI;183)
27 Nov.1801,	"		Rebecca Robertson
5 Sept.1814,	George		Maria F.Smith dau.of Frederick
25 Oct.1784,	Nathaniel		Eliz.Marriott,(W.B.V;316)
12 Apr.1843, Robins	Alfred A.		Indiana J.C.Pritchett dau.of Joseph S.
6 Oct.1848,	Solomon		Mary F.Mize
2 Dec.1763,	* *		Lucy Fox dau.of William(W.B.IV;387)
17 Jan.1748, Robinson	* *		Cordelia Phenix dau.of Abram(W.B.II;181)
* Dec.1751,	George		Anne Irby wid.of John(O.B.IV;143)
2 Dec.1763,	* *		Lucy Fox dau.of William(W.B.IV;387)
31 Oct.1827,	Bennet		Pamela S.Wilson
29 Jan.1749,	George		Ann Irby widow of John
13 Jan.1838,	" W.		Lucy E.G.Manning dau.of John
3o Sept.1770,	Henry		Mary Clack[dau.of John],Edward Robinson sec .
27 Feb.1761,	James		Winifred Fox, William Fox sec.
22 Dec.1808	John		Eliza P.Clack, Edward Thrower sec.
23 Jan.1815,	"		Eliz.Stith (O.B.XXVI;197)
25 Nov.1790,	Littleberry		Sally Robinson dau.of John
23 Oct.1769,	Nathaniel		Eliz.Merrit, Thomas Mason sec.
23 Sept.1839,	Richard B.		Isabella Dromgoole
14 Feb.1848,	Samuel H.		Lucy Ann Mallory dau.of Alexander

4 Apr.1844, Robinson, William H.   to Sally Epperson

30 Apr.1777,   * *   Franky Jones dau.of Isaac(W.B.V;15)

8 Jan.1835, Rodgers, George L.   Sarah D.Williams

9 Sept.1754,Rogers   * *   Katherine Proctor dau.of Robert(W.B.III;
                                                                                263)
11 Nov.1837,   Benjamin H.   Sarah G.Davis dau.of James decd.

23 Nov.1805,   George   Eliz.Nolly, Neremiah Nolly consent.

22 Oct.1787,   John   Mary Richardson dau.of Thomas

13 Feb.1806,   "   Sally Zachry

3 Mar.1795, Rollins,   * *   Agness Pritchett dau.of William(W.B.VI;

12 Dec.1798,   * *   Polly Abernathy dau.of James(W.B.VI;206)

3 May 1796, Rook,   * *   Olive Read dau.of James

29 Sept.1813,   Daniel   Santhy Huff

23 Dec.1785, Roper,   Jeremiah   Patsy Wilson dau.of John,Moses Quarles
                                                                                sec.
23 Dec.1811, Rose,   Henry   Martha Malone

28 Jan.1775,   John   Eliz.Davis dau.of Benjamin

7 Dec.1801   "   Betsy Talley

18 Dec.1812,   Lewis   Sarah Birdsong

23 Dec.1801,   William   Eliz.Meredith dau.of David

15 Dec.1807, Ross,   Daniel   Betsy Wyche

15 Oct.1828,   Peter W.   Eliz.B.Green

3 Nov.1778, Rosser,   David   Betty Reives, Banjamin Reives sec.

11 Oct.1796,   * *   Susan Gee dau.of William (W.B.VI;73)

6 Oct.1753, Rotenberry,Richard   * * Nipper dau.of John(W.B.III;83)

2 Dec.1742,   John   Susanna Williamson dau.of John(D.B.II;
                                                                                204)
9 Oct.1796, Rouse,   Peter   Sarah Laurence dau.of Robert decd.

21 July 1758,Rowell,   Edward   Betty Shelton ward of Edward Rowell

26 Nov.1842, Rowlett,	Thomas M	to	Amanda E.A.Lucy
26 July 1787,Ruffin,	Benjamin		Sara Edmunds dau.of Nicholas(W.B.V;298)
6 Sept.1751,	Robert		Molly Lightfoot widow,⌊dau.of Jas.Clack⌋
4 Nov.1831,	Thomas		Louisa S.Gilliam
11 Jan.1803, Russel,	Henry		Lucretia Laffoon
12 July 1758,	John		Sarah Edmundson, Thomas Twitty sec.
25 Dec.1804,	Matthew		Nancy Barnes
29 Aug.1794,	* *		Eliz.Strange dau.of Owen(W.B.V;559)
17 May 1836, Sadler,	Benjamin		Angelica M.Pritchett dau.of Edmund
3 Feb.1835,	" L		Pheobe Avery
22 Feb.1841,	Charles A.		Agness C.Pritchett dau.of Edmund
14 Sept.1848,	" "		Rebecca L.Duggar,
26 May 1794,	Edward F.		Mary Rose, Washington Craft sec.
8 Oct.1823,	Featherston		Catherine Lewis dau.of Ruel
26 Jan.1810,	Henry		Polly Vaughan
7 Aug.1780,	* *		Martha Rose dau.of John (.W.B.V;123)
29 Dec.1841,	Henry		Martha Scoggin dau.of John
24 Feb.1800,	John		Betsy Williams
10 Dec.1832,	"		Maria S.Floyd dau.of Clarissa
18 Dec.1848,	" F.		Mary F.Anderson dau.of Carter R.
6 Jan.1840,	Thomas A.		Sarah P.Pritchett
30 Sept.1828,	" F.		Mary W.Browder
29 Mar.1841,	Willington J.		Rebecca Gee
9 Feb.1819, Salmon,	John B.		Eliz.Barner dau.of John Jr.
20 May.1848, Samford,	Alex.E.M.		Lucy J.Smith dau.of Lucy N.

12 July 1791, Samford,   James   to   Ellen Johnson, John Johnson sec.

31 May .798,   "   Patsy

21 Oct.1824,   "   Catherine Newsum

3 Dec.1814,   John   Martha M.Bishop

28 Apr.1787,   Joseph   Milly Burks dau.of George, John Minor
                                                          sec.

17 Dec.1842,   Watkins   Susan A.E.Bishop

26 Dec.1785, Sanders,   John   Peggy Pentecost, John Williams sec.

25 Mar.1815, Saunders, Edward C. Polly P.Underhill dau.of John

23 Oct.1801,   John   Susan Williams

18 Mar.1805,   "   Dolly W.Ezell dau.of Buckner

4 Dec.1795,   Joseph   Patsey Maclin, Frederick Maclin sec.

5 May 1798,   Lewis   Martha Saunders

19 Dec.1836,   Sterling Mary Cooksey

2 April 1818,   Thomas   Eliz.Jones

22 July 1799,   Turner   Frances Dunn dau.of Ishmael

28 May 1808,   William   Patsey Lane

22 Apr.1833,   "   Eliz.Gibbs

28 Oct.1798, Scarbrough, Enos,   Nancy Neal

15 Sept.1800,   Sterling Mary Reece dau.of Isham

13 Jan.1798,   William   Eliz.Samford

17 Dec.1814, Scoggin, Benjamin A. Martha Abernathy

29 Feb.1788,   Gardner   Martha Lucy dau.of Robert,Robt Dunkley
                                                     sec.

28 Jan.1809,   Henry   Loisa Brown

18 Dec.1798,   John   Nancy Abernathy

26 Oct.1831,   "   Mary A.Birdsong

30 Oct.1835,   Manson,   Jane Moore

23 July 1821, Scoggin	Robert	to	Eliz.E.Williams
10 Dec.1796,	William		Polly Crook, Jiles Crook sec.
21 Apr.1792,	* *		Patty Lucey dau.of Robert(W.B.V;480)
26 Nov.1838, Scott,	Edward C.		Marenda F.Moore,
13 July 1820,	George B.		Polly Wynne
17 May 1808,	Henry E.		Sarah Edmunds dau.of Thomas
25 Aug.1834,	Peter E.		Harriett Meade dau.of Mary
27 Nov.1838,	Thomas F.		Martha M.Bass
19 Mar.1769, Seawell,	Benjamin		Lucy Hicks dau.of Sarah (W.B.IV;26)
9 Nov.1795, Sedbury,	John		Polly Davis, Truford Harvey sec.
28 Jan.1822, Selden,	Edward B.		Ann E.J.Hinton, Robert Turnbull sec
16 Dec.1828, Seward,	Cargill B.		Ann C.Kidd dau.of Joseph.
1 Dec.1825,	Hinchia		Frances Johnson dau.of Lewis & Lucretia
9 Dec.1845,	Hugh L.		Mary E.House
24 Feb.1834,	James		Jane Ezell
17 Sept.1838,	" R.		Eliz.C.Ezell niece of Buckner B.Ezell
9 Sept.1848,	" Ruffin		Eliz.C.Wesson
4 Dec.1804,	John		Nancy Taylor
27 July 1807,	"		Lucy Thrower
26 Aug.1833,	" W.		Mary S.Pearson
29 Oct.1824,	Joseph,		Martha King dau.of C.King Sr.
13 Jan.1831,	Richard B.		Lucy F.B.King dau.of John
9 Jan.1828,	Ruffin		Martha G.Jones dau.of William
15 Nov.1802,	William		Franky Thrower
16 Feb.1773, Sexton,	* *		Mary Brown dau.of Richard (W.B.IV;148)
12 Dec.1798,	Benjamin		Martha Abernathy dau.of James

9 Dec.1837, Seymour,	John H. to	Theophane R.Rose dau.of Henry
27 June 1831,	Mansfield R.	Sarah Ann King
14 Dec.1808,	William	Lucy Rose
12 Dec.1803, Ahadborne,	William S.	Sarah Barker
9 Dec.1795, Shell,	Edmunds	Patsy Lane 21,dau.of Benjamin
7 Aug.1813,	Green	Polly Moseley,
17 Feb.1795,	John	Betsy Turner, Edmund Shell sec.
13 Mar.1793, Shelton,	Daniel	Charlotte Mausback
16 Mar.1795,	"	Charlotte Stainback dau.of William (?)
6 June 1836,	"	Mary Jane Ogburn
20 Aug.1825,	George P.	Martha S.Harwell dau.of John H.
9 Dec.1825,	Thomas	Susan Peebles
15 Dec.1828, Short,	Alexander M.	Antionette Zimmer dau.of Lewis.
12 Feb.1800,	Anderson	Mabel Short
5 Feb.1833,	" W.	Amanda E.O.Harrison
31 Oct.1798,	Benjamin	Frances Howze, Merrit Huze sec.
20 Dec.1837	Charles M.	Susan J.Winn
23 Dec.1837,	Cincivantus	Ann C.Perkins
26 Sept.1804,	Edmund	Nancy Lanier
27 Nov.1843,	George	Mary Jane Mallory
21 Oct.1829,	" C.	Eliz.Matthews dau.of Samuel
27 Dec.1805,	Griffin	Rebecca Short
26 Dec.1814,	"	Abby Abernathy dau.of John
9 Dec.1840,	"	Martha C.Dameron
6 Dec.1844,	Henry A.	Maryland R.Mathews dau.of Francis P.
11 Dec.1841,	John A.	Martha Mathews dau.of Samuel

20 May 1819, Short,	John T.	to	Eliz.Abernathy
28 Sept.1807,	Major		Polly Adams
5 June 1820,	"		Rebecca Ridout
27 Feb.1830,	William		Martha B.Harris
27 Dec.1802,	Willie		Frances F.Harrison
22 Apr.1844,	"		Lucy Ann Smith
21 Apr.1792,	* *		Sally Lucey dau.of Robert (W.B.V;480)
18 July 1837, Sills,	Joshua,		Eliz.A.Orgain
16 Nov.1772, Simmons,	Benjamin		Sarah Butts dau.of John
24 Dec.1773,	"		Martha Embrey, Peter Pelham Jr.sec.
3 Feb.1762,	* *		Sarah Samford dau.of William(W.B.IV;317)
11 Apr.1797,	* *		Ann Jean Lundie dau.of Thomas(W.B.VI;133
23 Sept.1822, Simpson,	Arthur J.		Mary C.Dromgoole
14 June 1745, Sims,	⌊Adam⌋		Tabitha Jackson dau.of Ambrose(W.B.II;109)
16 Nov.1796,	Herbert		Nancy Wade, James Wade sec.
28 Nov.1785,	Howell		Lucy George dau.of Enoch
18 July 1799,	"		Delphia Rogers dau.of John
* * *	"		Lucy George dau.of Enoch
24 Nov.1806,	Millenton		Eliz.Thrower
6 Mar.1799,	Richard		Rebecca Droomgoole
24 Apr.1770,	William		Eliz.Wall dau.of Michael & Rebecca
19 Dec.1835, Singleton,	Edmund		Sally J.Taylor
3 Jan.1787,	James		Patsey Bailey, James Thompson sec
5 June 1826,	John		Herison Foster
15 Nov.1837,	"		Martha Floyd
23 Sept.1844,	" J.		Mary Smith

29 July 1789, Singleton,   William to Leicee Morris dau.of Thomas(W.B.V;324)

25 Aug.1794, Sison,   * *   Sarah Strange dau.of Owen(W.B.V;559)

3 June 1736, Sisson   Thomas   Hannah Raines dau.of John of Surry(1;268)

21 Jan.1815, Slate,   John   Polly Tarpley

20 Dec.1819,   "   Tabitha Huff dau.of Lewis

27 Aug.1842,   " J.   Harriet S.Thommason dau.of Bannister

28 Oct.1841,   Peterson   Harrietta C.Delbridge dau.of Warren

26 Nov.1792,   Randolph   Amey King, Isham Smith sec.

* Nov.1785,   Robert   Sally Turner dau.of John, Lewis Brown
                                                           sec.

13 Dec.1819,   " W.   Rebecca Birdsong

7 Dec.1815,   William   Martha Harris

26 Dec.1811, Sledge,   Miles C.   Sally Jordan

24 July 1786,Smith,   Abraham   Lucy Raines dau.of James, Joshua Lucy
                                                           sec.

3 Dec.1845,   Albert J. Rebecca J.Walker

25 Oct.1773,   Benjamin   Nancy Burch

26 Apr.1802,   "   Martha Fort

14 Dec.1830,   " J.   Lucy N.Ogburn dau.of John

12 Dec.1800,   Bolling   Lovey Owens

25 July 1758,   Cuthbert   Eliz.Lanier widow[of Sampson]

21 Oct.1807,   "   Joanna D.Neal [dau.of John & Susan]

24 Oct.1802,   Clement   Patsy Slate

29 Jan.1770,   David   Ruth Pattway dau.of John (W.B.IV;10)

27 Nov.1809,   "   Rebecca Bass

8 Dec.1824,   Douglass   Frances Singleton dau.of Randolph

22 May 1780,   Eads   Mary Davis, John Morris sec.

12 June 1821,   Edward   Eliz.L.Kirk

27 Aug.1838, Smith,	Edward C.	to Ariana W.Hungerford dau.of Helen W.
15 Nov.1787,	Fred	Mary Brodnax, Henry Jackson sec.
2 Jan.1804,	Fred'k	Nancy Sims
26 Nov.1810,	Gabriel	Polly Burks
13 July 1807,	George	Caroline Hunnicutt dau.of Benjamin
14 May 1830,	" J.	Martha Maclin dau.of Joseph
8 June 1790,	James	Nancy Gargus, Hamlin Freeman sec.
11 June 1798,	"	Lucy Fort, Edwin Fort sec.
21 Feb.1814,	"	Maria Lucy dau.of Robert
11 Dec.1820,	"	Eliz.Keen Bishop dau.of John
24 Dec.1826,	"	Eliz.Slate
4 Oct.1847,	" C.	Mary A.E.Short
24 Nov.1794,	John	Priscilla Perry, Cary James sec.
24 Jan.1803,	"	Ritta Nanny
5 Oct.1804,	"	Sally Walton
4 Feb.1805,	" B.	Letitia Keats
27 Oct.1834,	" H.	Eliza A.Moody
11 Dec.1841,	" H.	Sarah W.Ogburn
27 Feb.1832,	Joseph H.	Louisa Hampton dau.of David
11 Dec.1798,	Lewis	Sally Capell
17 Oct.1791,	Millington	Betsey Mathews dau.of Lucy
2 Jan.1799,	Pleasant	Polly Thompson
12 Nov.1821,	"	Eliz.Buckner
24 Nov.1823,	Richard	Ann Lett niece of John Lett
19 Jan.1830,	"	Rebecca Walton
29 Oct.1830,	"	Prudence Adams

110

7 Sept.1835, Smith,	Richard to	Susan M.Sadler dau.of Henry
6 Jan.1837,	" E.C.	Helen A.Hungerford
18 Sept.1806,	" S.	Frances Moore dau.of Sterling
6 Aug.1827,	Sherwood	Frances Avenhunt
25 May 1778,	Stephen	Olive Harrison dau.of Nathaniel
8 Sept.1828,	" A.	Louisa Dromgoole,ward of Edw.Dromgoole
27 Nov.1869,	Sterling W.	Nancy Hartwell
25 July 1803,	William	Betsy Williams
17 Dec.1809,	"	Sally Hogwood
28 Oct.1839,	"	Mary E.Webb
13 Aug.1828,	" A.	Eliz.C.T.Seward dau.of Lucy C.
28 Oct.1833,	" B.Dr.	Mildred M.Bolling, Ann Bolling's con.
18 Jan.1830,	" L.B.	Sarah Smith
17 Mar.1757,	* * *	Pheobe Livesey dau.of William(W.B.III;215)
14 June 1769,	* * *	Lucy Ward dau.of John(W.B.III;356)
8 July 1771,	* * *	Eliz. Collier dau.of Isaac (W.B.IV;80)
25 Mar.1794,	* * *	Polly Harrison dau.of Nath.(W?B.VI; 63)
26 Mar.1794,	* * *	Dolly Harrison dau.of Nath.(W.B.VI;64)
3 May 1796,	* * *	Anne Harrison dau.of Nath.(W.B.VI;66)
25 Sept.1815,Smily,	Jesse,	Eliza R.Harrison
24 Oct.1825, Sneed,	Hamilton	Martha C.Dunnivant
13 Sept.1831,Southall,	Thomas	Susan S.Simms
17 May 1767, Sparkes,	* *	Tabitha Sexton (W.B.III;535)
24 Sept.1838,Speaks,	Edwin	Dianotia P.Hudson dau.of Gregory B.
14 June 1759,Spearman,	* *	Mary Ward dau.of John (W.B.III;356)
26 May 1796, Speed,	* *	Eliz.Mason dau.of Sarah(W.B.VI;57)

27 July 1801,	Speers,	James, to	Rody Moseley
17 Apr.1801,	Spencer,	John	Rebecca Stith
12 Mar.1773,		Robert	Mary Charles dau.of Lewis
11 Oct.1828,		Thomas E.	Lucretia B.Walker
26 Mar.1810,	Spicely,	James,	Ann King
16 Feb.1829,		"	Martha Edwards
7 Mar.1836,	Stainback,	Ashley D.	Catherine E.Palmer dau.of William
22 Dec.1783,		Francis	Sarah Hardaway, William Caudle sec.
10 Sept.1785,		"	Nancy Bass dau.of Thomas
25 Mar.1816,		George J.	Susan Atkerson dau.of Sarah
11 May 1816,		Henry	Susan Boswell widow
14 Dec.1795,		James	Eliz.Duggar, Richmond Duggar sec.
20 Dec.1785,		John	Mary Powell dau.of John
27 July 1840,		" C.	Indiana Mason dau.of N.
27 Dec.1833,		" E.	Mary A.J.Williams
24 Feb.1792,		Robinson	Jincy Davenport dau.of Mary,John Owen sec.
19 Dec.1826,		Robert A.	Lucy Bass
28 Dec.1849,		William R.	Julia E.Edwards
7 Apr.1756,		* *	Nancy Bass dau.of Thomas(W.B.V;168)
15 Mar.1802,		* *	Lucy Robinson dau.of Edward(W.B.VI;473)
6 Apr.1802,		* *	Louisa Duggar dau.of John
2 July 1793,	Stamper,	Robert	Keziah Bagwell, Moses S.Hampton sec.
25 Jan.1796,	Standley,	James	Sally Ezell, Benjamin Ezell sec.
14 Jan.1824,	Stanley	Benjamin	Francis Preston dau.of Joshua.
28 Mar.1787,	Starke,	Lewis	Dionasia Jones [dau.of Peter]
14 Dec.1831,		Peter B.	Adeline Kirkland

4 Oct.1834, Starke,	William E.to	Louisa G.Hicks
4 Dec.1830, Steed,	Abner J.	Martha J.King dau.of Miles
15 Oct.1800,	Jonathan	Eliz.Huff 21 years
24 Nov.1817,	Thomas H.	Eliz.E.Barker dau.of Burwell
24 Feb.1772, Stegall,	Thomas	Eliz.Ingram exx.of John I.Jr.(O.B.XI;501)
27 Nov.1774, Step,	* *	Susanna Clark dau.of Joshua(W.B.IV;244)
16 Apr.1804, Steward,	Richard	Charlotte James dau.of Bob
1 Oct.1806, Stewart,	Armistead	Flora Cook (Chunky)
25 Mar.1833,	Pastors,	Fanny Magee
23 Jan.1830, Stegall,	Dudley G.	Amanda C.Scott dau.of Eliz.R.
25 Nov.1800,	George	Catherine Atkins
14 Mar.1818,	Ralph,	Lucinda Nolley
4 Nov.1833,	Thomas	Eliz.Walton dau.of William
20 May 1807, Stith,	Andrew	Polly Mathews dau.of John
* Feb.1786,	Buckner	Eliz.Jones
22 Sept.1788,	Drury	Fanny Love dau.of Allen decd.Thos.Stith sec.
15 May 1822,	"	Eliz.Short dau.of Mabel
9 Aug.1809,	Henry	Mary W.Spain dau.of William
20 Jan.1825,	"	Helen L.Goodwyn
24 June 1799,	John	Maria Meade dau.of Susanna,Buckner Stith sec .
2 May 1807,	"	Nancy Cary
31 Mar.1814,	" W.	Margaret C.Drummond dau.of John
20 July 1825,	Needum W.	Lucy G.Haskins
15 Apr.	Obediah	Mary L.Hunnicutt dau.of Benjamin
13 Dec.1847,	O.E.	Frances H.Smith

7 Aug.1780, Stith,	Thomas	to	Holly Bailey, William Rainey sec.
27 Nov.1786,	"		Susanna Harris dau.of Mathew
24 Sept.1756,	William		Katherine Stith, Drury Stith sec.
24 Aug.1756, Stokes,	Sylvanus Jr.		Temperence Clarke dau.of George
lo July 1805,	William,Dr.		Polly Harrison dau.of John
19 May 1824, Stone,	George,		Mary Ann Kirkland
2 Jan.1832,	Jason		Eliz.Elmore dau.of William
27 Jan.1803,	Jathan		Sally Dixon
19 Oct.1806,	"		Nancy Dixon
11 Aug.1807,	John		Vicy Simmons
6 Jan.1844,	" J.		Martha Epperson
27 Feb.1801,	Peter		Fanny Sammons
13 Apr.1843,	" R.		Ann J.Cole dau.of William
22 Mar.1784,	Richard		Delitha Gibbs, William Gibbs sec.
31 Dec.1763,	* *		Frances Read dau.of William(W.B.IV;393)
16 Sept.1771,	* *		Eliz.Threadgill dau.of John(W.B.IV;117)
23 Dec.1816, Strange,	Henry		Nancy Ferguson
4 Apr.1744,	Owen		Eliz.Sisson dau.of Thomas.(D.B.II;466)
5 Feb.1820,	William		Nancy Shelton dau.of Charlotte Strange.
24 Dec.1819, Stroud,	Thomas		Nancy M.Gordon
29 Nov.1752, Stuart,	James		Eliz.Irby, John Irby ssec.
2 Dec.1742, Sturdivant,	Hollum		Eliz.Williamson dau.of John.(D.B.II;204)
5 Apr.1793,	John		Susanna Collier, James Hicks Jr.sec.
25 Oct.1841,	Joseph Wm.		Juliette Coleman dau.of Nathaniel H.
15 Dec.1802,	William		Martha Cheely
7 Jan.1797, Suggett,	Benjamin		Nancy Sturdivant dau.of John

23 July 1789,	Suggett,	Edgcomb to	Molly Jones dau.of Stephen
22 July 1822,		"	Frances Rawlings dau.of Benjamin
3 Nov.1817,		Thomas	Lucy S.Bishop dau.of John
22 Aug.1796,	Talley,	Joel	Rebecca Rose 21 years,Robert Lattimore sec.
2 Nov.1799,		William	Rebecca Briggs, Frederick Briggs sec.
6 Oct.1835,		" G.	Manerva Lanier dau.of Thomas
19 July 1824,		" W.	Eliz.W.Judd
lo Dec.1819,	Tanner,	John A.	Minerva Thrower dau.of Mary
26 Jan.1801,	Tansil,	John	Betsy Collier
4 Aug.1800,	Tarpley,	Edward Jones	Mary B.Manson
15 Nov.1811,		Henry	Nancy Elmore
22 Sept.1833,		"	Rebecca Hill
19 June 1799,		Joel	Eliz.Johnson
21 Dec.1796,		John	Sally Barrow, dau.of William
16 Oct.1786,		Thomas	Sally Moore, Samuel Moore sec.
16 Feb.1773,		* *	Edna Brown dau.of Richard(W.B.IV;148)
6 Sept.1819,	Tarver,	John H.	Hannah Hill
5 Aug.1803,	Tarwater,	Michael	Caty Trotter dau.of George
10 Jan.1797,	Tatum,	Edward,	Mary Ogburn dau.of James
27 Feb.1797,		Herbert	Eliz.Ogburn
28 May..787,		Jesse	Polly Cook, Benjamin Warren sec.
27 Apr.1837,		Norfleet	Martha G.Seward
13 July 1797,		Osborne	Susanna Harwell
5 Jan.1799,		Sihon	Martha Ogborn

24 May 1803, Taylor,	Benjamin	to	Nancy Williams
15 Dec.1820,	"		Mary Ann C.Parham dau.of Thomas
20 Dec.1791,	Cornelius		Jane Haymour, Mark Haymour wit.
9 Dec.1805,	Daniel		Cresey Waller
11 Feb .1830,	"		Faithy Thomason dau.of William
19 Dec.1835,	George W.		Eveline G.Hawkins
25 Dec.1758,	Henry of So'n		Temperence Peterson dau.of John
14 Nov.1811,	"		Nancy Elmore
11 May 1831,	Herbert		Martha Scarbrough dau.of Sterling& Polly
2 Feb .1829,	Isaac		Eliz.J.Ryland
13 Dec.1833,	James		Lucy White dau.of John
3 Aug.1797,	Jesse		Lucretia Watson, George Watson sec.
5 Nov.1832,	" L.		Sarah S.Hawkins
22 July 1822,	" M.		Eliz.F.Rawlings
6 Aug.1790,	John		Aylce Atkins, John Atkins sec.
24 June 1800,	"		Polly C.Perry
28 Dec.1830,	" J.		Sally A.Walker
24 Feb.1823,	" W.		Eliz.J.W.Buckner
6 Dec.1803,	Jones		Jincy Mathews
1 Dec.1849,	Joseph C.		Martha Ann Mitchell
5 June 1849,	Leondias,		Frances J.Worthington dau.of M.M.
24 Dec.1792,	Lewis		Betsy Braswell, Jesse Braswell sec.
1 Dec.1804,	Mackey		Sally Taylor dau.of Daniel
8 Dec.1826,	Richard E.		Mary Clarke dau.of Joshua
20 Dec.1801,	Robert		Nancy Carpenter
24 May 1838,	"		Rebecca W.Chapman

12 Feb.1810,	Taylor,	Robert A.	to Margaret Saunders,
28 Apr.1798,		William	Susanna Singleton
22 Mar.1847,		" H.	Rosalie E.Harrison
10 Jan.1842,		" L.	Caroline E.Nanny dau.of Isaac
27 Mar.1817,	Temple,	Frederick,Pr.Geo.	Eliz.W.Mallory dau.of Roger
7 Feb.1801,	Tenesblum,	Thomas	Mary C.Holderby
23 Dec.1822,	Thacker,	James	Bathsheba Thacker dau.of Nancy
18 Dec.1788,		John	Nancy Overby, Reuel Lewis sec.
28 Nov.1825,		Robert K.	Emry B.Gee
13 Mar.1817,		Sterling	Mary H.Overby
16 Oct.1806,		William	Eliz.Dunkley
7 Sept.1805,	Thomas,	Allen	Theodicia Shell
25 Mar.1826,		Bennet	Nancy N.House
18 Nov.1822,		Charles	Sarah White dau.of John
22 Feb.1794,		Daniel	Milly Singleton 21, Henry Singleton sec.
18 Nov.1805,		David	Patsy Moseley
16 Aug.1848,		Edward	Harriet Mathews
18 Apr.1840,		Gabriel J.	Augusta Claiborne dau.of John G.
14 Oct.1786,		John	Sarah Laurence, Wood Laurence sec.
22 Dec.1817,		Lewis G.	Eliz. Rainey
23 Nov.1789,		Peter	Hannah Wall wid.of Henry,Thos.Stegall sec.
5 Nov.1791,		" Jr.	Martha Wall, ward of Peter Thomas Sr.
26 Dec.1803,		Richard	Patsey Moseley 21 yrs.
21 Nov.1836,		Robin	Quintina Hawkins dau.of Uriah
4 Oct.1845,		Stith	Rebecca J.Stainback
20 Aug.1820,		Thomas B.	Temperence Burge dau.of Pleasant

16 Feb.1820,Thomas,	Theophilus	to Lucy Pearson	
6 Apr.1738,	William	Margaret Duggar wid.of Richard(O.B.1; 191)	
16 Dec.1799,Thomason,	Banister	Polly Taylor	
24 May 1819,	Robert S.	Betsy Foster	
27 Nov.1826,	William	Catherine R.Bishop	
27 Dec.1847,	" R.E.	Lucy M.Williams	
27 Sept.1779,Tomlinson,	James	Eliz.Morris widow, William Robinson sec.	
20 Mar.1822,	John L.	Susan M.Newsom, Braxton Newsom cer.to age	
27 Nov.1820, Thompson,	Benjamin	Rebecca Walker dau.of Ann	
11 Jan.1802,	Darvill	Prissy Burge	
22 Dec.1783,	James	Sally Bell Quarles, William Roper sec.	
26 Nov.1827,	Benjamin	Ann Sims	
25 Mar.1815,	John	Rebecca Ann Davy	
5 Mar.1781,	Nathaniel	Eliz.Donaldson Dupree	
9 Aug.1837,	Peter	Ann E.Seymore dau.of William	
4 Nov.1737,	Richard	Eliz.Smith wid.of Patrick(O.B.1;176)	
9 June 1779,	* *	Abel Quarles dau.of Hubbard.(W.B.V;107)	
16 Feb.1774, Thornton,	William⌊Jr⌋	Sarah Goodrich dau.of Edward,John Clack sec.	
24 Dec.1783, Threadgill,Randle		Susanna Smith dau.of James	
24 Sept.1781,Thrower,	Christopher	Sally Sims dau.of John deceased.	
8 Nov.1847,	Edward	Rebecca Hicks	
26 Oct.1844,	Hezekiah D.	Mary Tillman	
15 Dec.1815,	John B.	Martha Meredith	
17 May1819,	" "	Ann E.House	
20 Oct.1835,	" "	Evalina H.Thrower dau.of Christopher	
19 May.1810, Thweatt, Thomas		Mary Ann Coleman	

118

 9 Dec.1799, Tilman,   Blumer   to Sally High

21 Aug.1797,   Jarratt   Lucretia Fann

23 May 1758,   John   Mary Simmons, John Daniel sec.

19 Oct.1770,   * *   Ann Randle dau.of William sr.(W.B.IV;67)

27 Aug.1810,   John   Sally Ryland

 4 Jan.1745, Timmons,   Prudence Mattox, (O.B.II;129)

17 Feb.1816, Tisdale,   Sherley   Ann E.C.Blick dau.of James

 9 Sept.1754,Towns,   * *   Priscilla Proctor dau.of Robert (W.B.III;
                                                                         265)

27 Apr.1792, Traylor,   Joseph,   Mary Jackson, Peter Wynne sec.

23 Sept.1833,   Robert   Martha Taylor

 6 Dec.1799, Trice,   Thomas   Sarah Hill

 9 Nov.1802, Trotter,   Benjamin   Mary S.Brown

16 Dec.1772,   George   Caty Crook dau.of Joseph,James Trotter
                                                                           sec.

27 Oct.1804,   "   Mary B.Hightower

 4 May 1832,   Henry   Margaret Rice

22 Nov.1773,   Isham   Jenny Burch, William Lanier sec.

27 May 1795,   "   Eliz.Whitehead dau.of Benjamin

13 Sept.1781,   James Sr.   Hannah Wilson,sec.Isham Trotter

28 Apr.1795,   "   Caty Keatts dau.of James

18 Jan.1801,   "   Eleann Rose

27 Jan.1803,   "   Lucy Pritchett

27 Oct.1794,   Richard   Eliz.Trotter, George Trotter sec.

11 Mar.1799,   Thomas   Polly S.Quarles

 6 Sept.1799,   William   Lucy Fowlkes dau.of Thomas

11 Sept.1784,   * *   Betsy Quarles dau.of James (W.B.V;400)

10 Feb.1838, Tucker,   Benjamin   to   Martha A.E.Sturdivant dau.of William

28 June 1836,   Edward B.   Mary Eliza Cumming

21 Dec.1786,   Frederick   Polly Crowder, Epharim Jackson sec.

11 Nov.1815   George   Martha Williams

25 July 1838,   Joseph   Minerva O.Turbyfill

18 June 1816,   Joseph St.George Martha House

 7 Feb.1849,   " J.G.   Lucy Tatum

24 Feb.1845,   Legrand M.   Eliz.E.Duane dau.of Timothy

 1 May 1825,   Nathaniel   Lucy M.J.Vaughan

 7 Jan.1804,   Sterling   Mary Ann Ingram

24 June 1833,   "   H.   Martha R.Field

 4 June 1841,   Robert R.   Martha F.Brown

17 Oct.1835,   Thomas Goode   Eliz.Lewis

26 Apr.1848,   William   Virginia M.Lewis

 5 Mar.1784,   Wright   Eliz.Williamson dau.of Charles

27 Oct.1827, Tudor,   Richard   Ann W.Birthright

27 Dec.1811, Turbyfill, Wilson   Jean Short

17 Jan.1842,   Richard W.   Ariana R.J.Harrison

25 Nov.1796,   Littleberry   Martha Conneley, Seth Turbyfill sec.

14 Mar.1812,   Nathaniel   Olive H.Smith dau.of Stephen

 8 Apr.1784,   Seth   Dolly King dau.of Charles

14 Dec.1785   William   Rebecca Scarbrough,Henry Andrews sec.

 5 Nov.1832,   "   Cornelia A.Smith

21 June 1837,Turnbull, Charles   Sarah E.Lashley

19 Apr.1827,   Peter J.⌊ones⌋   Catherine A?Maclin dau.of John D.

23 Nov.1801,   Robert   Eliz.J⌊ones⌋ Stith

23 Nov.1829, Turnbull,   Robert H. to Martha J.Crighton

 9 May 1774, Turner,   (Arthur)   Eliz.Donaldson dau.of Benjamin C.

19 Apr.1791,   Benjamin   Eliz.Clack 21 years,James Clack sec.

 4 Dec.1849,   "   P.   Mary S.Thompson

30 Dec.1812,   David   Ann Jones

 2 Jan.1829,   James   Eliz.L.Montgomery

 7 Feb.1784,   Jesse   Ann Meredith, Thomas Stone sec.

13 Feb.1797,   Mathew J.   Wilmouth Malone

27 July 1846,   Richard W.   Mary H.Smith

25 July 1769,   Simon   Lucy Little wid.of John (O.B.XI;159)

 7 Aug.1746, Twitty,   Thomas   Mary Wyatt wid.of Henry (O.B.III;65)

28 Oct.1822, Underhill,   Robert H.   Sally V.House dau.of Green T.

 5 Nov.1818 Vaden,   Isham W.   Nancy Walpole

11 Nov.1846, Vaiden   Henry M.   Adelia L.Rose

25 Nov.1825, Valentine,   Jones J.   Phebe Walton

25 Feb.1818,   Thomas   Sophia Quenshet (?)

15 Apr.1816, Vaughan,   Averett   Eliz.Ogburn

28 Feb.1829,   Benjamin   Martha H.Collier

26 Jan.1818,   "   J.   Eliz.Burnett

 9 May 1805,   Binns   Nancy Williams

17 Oct.1781,   David   Hannah Hightower wid.,Richard Vaughan
                                                                         sec.
26 Nov.1787,   "   Hannah Lester dau.of Andrew(O.B.XIV;604)

21 Dec.1785,   Herrod,   Dicey McKenny, John Dunkley sec.

14 Mar.1820,   "   Sarah Vaughan dau.of John H.

27 Oct.1783,   James   Mary Malone dau.of George,H.Bailey sec.

26 Mar.1804, Vaughan,	James	to	Polly Bass
3 Jan.1807,	"		Susanna Garrott
10 Jan.1809,	" H.		Rebecca Drake
26 Sept.1791,	Jeremiah		Martha Stegall, Thomas Stegall sec.
9 Jan.1804,	John H.		Rebecca Drake
24 Dec.1804,	Leveston		Sally Allen
10 Oct.1791,	Micajah		Delila McKenny, William McKenny sec.
25 Sept.1816,	"		Dicey Walker widow
11 July 1800,	Moody		Polly Lett
16 Nov.1801,	Richard		Tabitha Edwards, dau.of Jesse
26 June 1797,	Stephen		Sucky Rideout
24 Nov.1795,	William		Patsey Berry, William Meredith sec.
26 July 1802,	"		Tempy Emmery
20 June 1806,	" Capt.,		Peggy Rice
23 Mar.1812,	"		Hannah Bruce dau.of James
24 Apr.1837,	" H.		Ann E.Vaughan dau. of Robert
22 Dec.1840,	" "		Mary W.Griffin
5 Dec.1842,	" J.		A.B.Morris
12 Dec.1843,	" W.		Sally Ann Epperson dau.of David
3 Mar.1762,	* * *		Eliz.Ingram dau.of John (W.B.IV;376)
2 Sept.1766,	* * *		Mary Simmons dau.of Peter,(W.B.III;491)
19 Oct.1801,	* * *		Polly Duggar dau.of John (W.B.VI;389)
23 Dec.1811, Verrell,	Benjamin		Jane T.Abernathy
15 July 1830,Vick,	John A.		Mary Woodruff
8 Oct.1838,	Tamlin		Sarah Malone dau.of James
22 Apr.1793,	William		Eliz.Powell, John Stainback sec.

16 Aug.1760, Vincent,	* * *	to	Sarah Brewer dau.of George, (W.B.III;344)
23 Nov.1772,	John		Rebecca Wall dau.of Michael (O.B.XII;155
19 July 1785,Wade,	* *		Rebecca Moseley dau.of Benjamin (W.B.V; 140)
31 Jan.1799,	David		Betsy Williams dau.of Alexander
10 Apr.1843,	Thomas		Harriet S.Lanier
10 Dec.1827,Wainright,	Kennon H.		Ann C.Lockett
20 Feb.1787, Walker,	Alexander		Sarah Elliott dau.of Richard
15 Feb.1793,	"	(?)	Wilmouth Jones dau.of Peter
8 Mar.1824,	Arthur		Clancy Walker
5 Dec.1816,	Benjamin		Sarah W.Vaughan
31 May 1786,	David		Mary Elliott, Richard Elliott sec.
15 Dec.1806,	"		Eliz.Hardaway
6 Sept.1824,	" A.		Verenda S.Newman
6 Nov.1820,	Edward		Emma A.Newman
5 Feb.1840,	Edwin		Martha A.Poyner
27 Dec.1819,	Freeman		Mary Ann Manson
2 Dec.1819,	George		Dorothy Simms
24 Aug.1829,	"		Martha Tarpley
* Dec.1785,	Henry		Martha Winfield, Edward Walker sec.
18 May 1805,	Jesse		Dicey Wesson
15 Dec.1828,	John A.		Mary F.Palmer dau.of William
27 Feb.1819,	" M.		Lucy G.Jones
10 Mar.1833,	Moses		Harriet Smith bound girl to M.Edmunds
6 Dec.1811,	Robert		Abby Jones dau.of Libby
15 Dec.1813,	" F.		Catherine Hicks dau.of John

10 Oct.1842, Walker,   Thomas P. to Mary J.Smith dau.of George

11 Dec.1840,   " W.   Nancy Eldridge

26 Nov.1772,   William   Anne Harrison, Benjamin Harrison sec.

21 Dec.1791,   "   Agness Birchett dau.of Edward

21 Nov.1797,   "   Nancy V.Hicks

28 July 1817,   "   Harriet Walker dau.of Nancy V.

17 Feb.1812,   " Jr.   Rebecca Hicks dau.of John

25 Oct.1784,   Wilson   Angelica Mathews, Mark Steed sec.

19 Jan.1748, Wall,   * *   Martha Vaughan dau.of Richard(W.B.II; 165)

29 Sept.1788,   * *   * * Brodnax dau.of Ann,(W.B.V;285)

11 Feb.1822,   Edward   Eliza Smith, Thomas Clark gdn.

28 Jan.1795,   George   Martha House, Henry Wall sec.

25 Feb.1826,   Henry   Fanny M.Hull

* June 1752,   John   Mary Brown wid.of Capt.Burwell Brown. (O.B.IV;221)

22 June 1807,   "   Levinia Cole, William Edw.Brodnax sec.

3 Dec.1745,   Michael Jr.   Rebecca Chapman wid.of John.D.B.III;111)

6 Sept.1797,Wallace,   Jesse   Faithy Walpole, William Walpole sec.

27 May 1797,   John   Ruth Edwards dau.of John(W.B.VI;147)

20 Apr.1829,   William   Eliza E.H.Holloway

17 Dec.1832, Waller,   Garret   Henrietta S.Wynne dau.of Robert

14 June 1828,   Isaac H.   Rebecca C.Singleton

21 Nov.1805, Walpole,   Benjamin   Sally Johnson, William Johnson con.

23 Dec.1805,   John   Polly James

20 June 1798,   Richard   Agness Freeman

3 Oct.1789,   William   Lucy Johnson dau.of John,Thos.Goodrum sec.

23 May 1840, Walthall,   Edward B.   Pamelia Denton

2 Apr.1822, Walton,	Benjamin B.to	Eliz.Mitchell
22 Aug.1829,	David W.	Maria A.Pryor
27 Sept.1785,	Drury	Gracey Ingram dau.of Joseph,Jos.Ingram sec.
26 Jan.1789,	Elias Rowe	Mary Britt, Henry Britt sec.
27 Nov.1826,	" R.	Tabitha Woolsey
22 Apr.1817,	George	Patsey Williams
24 July 1815,	Hinchia M.	Eliz.Walton
28 Feb.1842,	Isaac R.	Frances E.Green dau.of Allen Jones Green
13 Mar.1797,	John	Polly Warwick 21 years
28 Aug.1848,	" R.	Martha A Taylor
23 Apr.1806,	Joshua	Susanna E.Hicks
25 Aug.1834,	Joshua	Hannah H.Richardson
8 Feb.1828,	Richard H.H.	Emma A.C.Hartwell
24 May 1830,	R.H.H.	Louisa S.Hartwell
24 Nov.1824,	Row	Lucy R.Williams
24 Sept.1798,	Thomas	Eliz.Porch dau.of Thomas,John Watson sec.
1 Aug.1786,	"	Mary Skinner, Henry Walton sec.
16 Dec.1802,	William	Luty Britt dau.of Benjamin
11 Feb.1836,	" H.	Martha Frayser
25 Sept.1786, Ward,	Richard	Winny Smith, William Ward sec.
23 Dec.1795,	Willie	Middy Smith, Cary James sec.
27 Jan.1784, Warden,	James	Lucy Hall, Briggs Goodrich sec.
7 Apr.1819, Wamsley,	James	Eliz.S.Watson
7 Apr.1756, Warren,	* *	Tempey Bass dau.of Thomas (W.B.V;168)
27 July 1778,	Benjamin	Tempe Bass, John Jeter sec.
19 Dec.1771(?)	Wiley Prince	Eliz.Payne

19 Dec.1791, Warren,   Wiley Penn, to   Eliz.Hayne, John Johnson sec.

12 Dec.1808, Warwick,   William   Margaret Seward

13 Nov.1815,   "   Peggy Vaughan

23 Dec.1791, Washington,Gray   Nancy Harrison, Willie Harrison sec.

22 Nov.1784,   Thomas   Janet Love dau.of Allen Love,

27 Jan.1805,   Warner   Ariana Stith, Lawrence W.Stith sec.

17 Dec.1827, Watkins,   Benjamin   Rebecca Bishop

 7 Aug.1809,   Frederick   Christiana Gresham

 6 May 1794,   Henry W.   Ann Edmunds, John Orgain sec.

24 May 1831,   Thomas   Lucy G.Wyche

 5 Mar.1750, Ware   * *   Susanna Randle dau.of John(D.B.IV;125)

22 Feb.1739; Watson   * *   Rebecca Jackson dau.of John.(O.B.II;127

13 Aug.1798,   Henry   Rebecca Butler

 9 Dec.1789,   John   Lucretia Walton, George Walton sec.

29 Jan.1770,   William   Lucretia Pettway dau.of John(W.B.Iv;10)

 6 Dec.1847, Watts,   Gill W.   Minerva DuPriest

16 Aug.1828,   John   Frances Wesson

29 Aug.1783, Weatherby, Septimus   Sarah Myrick dau.of John Sr.

 9 Dec.1848, Weaver,   John T.   Eliz.Delbridge dau.of Warren

18 Dec.1779,   William   Rebecca Whitington, John Whitington sec.

24 July 1776,Webb,   * *   Rebecca Edwards dau.of Col.William

19 Oct.1835,   Charles   Mary A.Britton

26 Dec.1808,   Edmund   Nancy Floyd

20 Nov.1822,   Edward   Rebecca Blanch

26 Nov.1798,   James   Rebecca Pearson 21 years

22 Aug.1803,   "   Frances Hicks

15 Nov.1828, Webb,	James	to	Lucy Seward,
8 Sept.1835,	"		Sarah Green
1 Jan.1817,	" E.		Martha A.Floyd, James Preston sec.
28 Nov.1836,	" H.		Sarah A.Owen dau.of James
24 Aug.1801, Wellburn,	John		Eliz.Abernathy
20 Sept.1827,Wells,	Hailey		Rebecca Tinsbloom widow
28 Mar.1836,	Hartwell B.		Harriet B.Vaughan dau.of Robert
15 Feb.1819,	John		Margaret Tucker
13 Oct.1829,	Robinson T.		Eliz.Johnson
16 July 1800,	Thomas		Sally Lanier
24 Aug.1861,	William		Sally Gee dau.of Robert
7 Jan.1813, Wesson,	Abner		Sally Hall
4 Dec.1806,	Anderson,		Jincy Wesson
4 Dec.1799,	Buckner		Nancy House
26 Dec.1785,	Edward		Rebecca Nanny, Drury Nanny sec.
23 Dec.1805,	"		Jincy Williams dau.of ᴹary
18 Dec.1820,	Green		Nancy Delbridge dau.of Thomas
9 Dec.1811,	"		Sally Nicholson
19 Dec.1837,	Henry J.		Martha J.Wesson dau.of Isaac D
25 Dec.1809,	Isaac		Tabitha Seward dau.of Joseph
8 Mar.1823,	"		Tabitha J.Lucy widow
27 Apr.1818,	" D.		Delbridge(Lucy)
25 Mar.1839,	" "		Lucy L.Wesson dau.of John.
28 Jan.1788,	James		Nancy Clary dau.of Harwood, Reuben Wray sec.
9 Dec.1795,	John		Eliz.Jones, Jesse Jones sec.
12 Dec.1808,	"		Delila Massey

18 Dec.1835, Wesson,	John	to	Margaret L.Mason
3 Sept.1813,	Joseph		Eliz.Nicholson
4 Nov.1797,	Julius		Lucy Wesson, Henry Wesson sec.
23 Dec.1793,	Littleton		Betsy Justice 21 yrs. Thos.Wesson sec.
22 Dec.1794,	THomas		Lucy Kelly dau.of Moses
13 Nov.1798,	"		Nancy Jones
31 Mar.1809,	Washington		Cesley Pearson
31 May 1836,	William D.		Narcissa M.Bacon
29 Apr.1786,	"		Rebecca Roberts, Stephen Wesson sec.
27 Dec.1791,	"		Beckey Vaughan, David Blaylock sec.
16 Dec.1796,	Willie		Hannah Howard, James Wesson sec.
20 Dec.1794, West,	Epharim		Eliz.Ingram, Bartho.Ingram sec.
5 Dec.1842,	Henry G.		Jane Cole
24 Feb.1794,	John		Lucy Williams, Thomas Edmunds,J.P.
24 Feb.1795,	"		" " ,Lewis Holloway sec.
2 May 1826, Westmoreland, David			Sally Lucy
31 Mar.1823,	Hartwell		Polly Harris
25 Oct.1802,	Jesse		Eliz.G.Ingram
28 Dec.1801,	Peterson		Eliz.Jolly
26 Mar.1787,	Robert		Lucy Freeman dau.of Henry, S.Capel sec.
6 Oct.1753,	Thomas		* * Nipper dau.of John,(W.B.III;83)
23 June 1806,Wheeler,	Moses		Eliz.Carpenter
28 Jan.1793, Whitaker,	Robert L.		Sally Leadbetter, Henry Leadbetter sec.
25 Dec.1815, Whitt,	John		Frances Burrow,
7 Jan.1811, Whitby,	Elisha		Sally Wright
21 Dec.1842,	George		Jane W.Edwards

22 Nov.1819, Whitby,	Jordan	to	Judith Lane dau.of Simon
11 Dec.1809,	Robert		Middy Nanny
8 Aug.1844, White,	David		Roanna M.Farlow
6 June 1835,	Edwin		Althea Sturdivant dau.of E.C.
23 Dec.1830,	George		Ann Eliza Mason
14 Dec.1841,	" E.		Rebecca Ann Thomas dau.of Stith
18 May 1842,	James C.		Mⁿ. Argyra Blunt
22 Nov.1796,	John		Susanna Gunn, John Tillman sec.
15 Dec.1800,	"		Polly Steed
8 Feb.1803,	Stepher		Mary Hearn
20 Feb.1800,	Samuel		Nancy Barker
23 Mar.1846,	" M.		Cornelia A.Jackson
19 Dec,1821	Theophilus		Mary Jett 21 years
26 Nov.1795,	Valentine		Molly Cook, Frederick Cook sec.
3 June 1819,Whitlock,	Thomas		Sally Allen
26 Dec.1796, Whittey,	Burwell		Molly Nanny, John Nanny sec.
6 Mar.1790 Whittemore,William			Ann Adams, Gower Adams sec.
26 May 1806, Whittington,Lewis			Frances Brown
23 Dec.1771, Wilkins,	Douglas		Tabitha Sims dau.of Adam.(O.B.XI;430)
23 Dec.1771,	Edmund		Rebecca Sims dau.of Adam (" " ")
20 Oct.1790,	John L.		Katherine Stith, William Wilkins sec.)
5 Apr.1827,	" "		Ann Brodnax
20 Sept.1799,	Joseph		Eliz.B.Jones, George H.Jones sec.
28 Sept.1836,	Richard A.		Matilda F.Meade ward of R.Kidder M.
23 Luly.1839,	William Webb,Dr,Mary A.Beasley		
30 June 1841,	" W.		Louisa G.Lewis

14 May 1782, Wilkes,   Burwell   to Susanna Cordle, William Cordle sec.

11 AUG.1831,   "   B.   Lucy G.Field

26 Nov.1787,   John   Eliz.Stegall, George Stegall sec.

26 Jan.1795,   Joseph   Polly Jackson, Herbert Hill sec.

26 Nov.1787   Thomas   Mary Lester dau.of Andrew (O.B.XIV;206)

24 Nov.1823,Wilkinson, Benjamin   Mary W.Orgain

27 Dec.1843,   John P.   Mariah G.Hawkins

25 Oct.1807,   Robert   Polly, Robinson

17 Feb.1801,   Thomas   Biddy Browder

17 Dec.1786,   William   Eliz.Stainback, Robinson Stainback sec.

24 Mar.1836,   "   Capt.   Susan W.Gregg dau.of William

29 Dec.1821,   " B.   Mary C.Robinson

 7 Jan.1769, Williams, * * *   Eliz.Weaver dau.of John, W.B.III;530)

25 Nov.1778,   * * *   Eliz.Ledbetter,dau.of Mary.(W.B.V;58)

 7 Aug.1780,   * * *   Amey Rose dau.of John W.B.V;123)

20 July 1791,   * * *   Eliz.Clarke dau.of Elisha,(W.B.V;444)

17 Mar.1770,   Alexander   Eliz.Sims, William Sims sec.

27 Jan.1810,   Benjamin   Nancy Manly

21 Nov.1807,   Burwell   Lucy Lewis

22 Oct.1821,   Cary   Susan Mitchell

21 Dec.1796,   David   Dianah Edwards dau.of Jesse

16 Jan.1804,   "   Eliz.Ballentine

26 May 1806p   Edmond   Eliz.Williams

 * * 1820?   Edward   Jane K.B.Delbridge

 2 June 1808,   Garrett,   Winifred Lanier

29 Jan.1849,   Green   Rebecca Birdsong dau.of Nathaniel

6 Oct.1823, Williams,	Henry W.	to	Mary Harrison
10 Sept.1819,	Hugh H.		Eliz.F.Duggar
25 Jan.1802,	Isaac		Tabitha House
6 May 1798,	James		Rebecca Parker, John Parker con.
23 Jan.1843,	" D.		Croline G.Phillips
* Sept.1747,	John		Frances Wyatt dau.of Henry(
14 Nov.1781,	"		Mary Fowler dau.of Daniel (W.B.V;287)
22 Sept.1788,	"		Frances Strange dau.of Owen, John Moss sec.
26 Dec.1803,	"		Nancy Braswell
27 Mar.1805,	"		Betsey Bass
16 Dec.1809,	"		Nancy Betty
9 Jan.1826,	"		Mary Robinson
5 Oct.1816,	" R.		Martha D.Jones dau.of Robert
20 Jan.1846,	" L.		Martha J.Griffin
26 Dec.1786,	Jones		Eliz.Clark, Drury Stith sec.
24 Aug.1801,	"		Eliz.Evans dau.of Evan
21 Aug.1811,	"		Polly W.Davenport
25 May 1789,	Joseph		Frances Dailey wid. George Malone sec.
25 May 1811,	"		Sarah Williams
19 Apr.1838,	"		Ann S.Smiley
17 Dec.1846,	" E.		Sarah J.Phillips dau.of Benjamin M.
27 Apr.1789,	Lewelling		Eliz.Hagood, Gresham Hagood sec.
26 Jan.1825,	Littleberry		Martha J.Ogburn dau.of Benjamin
15 Oct.1819,	Marcum H.		Jane Harrison
12 Nov.1821,	Mathew of Meck.		Nancy T.Blanch, Ezekiel & Milly son.
28 Apr.1781,	Miles		Pricilla Hill dau.of William.

7 May 1821, Williams,	Miles		to Nancy Newsum dau.of Barham
15 Dec.1840,	Nathaniel		Susan Wray dau.of Anderson
22 May 1786,	Ozborne		Molly Dunn dau.of William,(O.B.XIV;336)
9 Mar.1804,	Robert		Tempy Wesson
3 Dec.1816,	"		E.Birdsong
20 Dec.1802,	"		Catherine S.Mann
19 Mar.1830,	"	H.	Nancy B.Walton
31 Dec.1832,	"	"	Henrietta C.Williams
21 Dec.1835,	"	"	Mary C.Harris,
21 June 1843,	"	J.	Julia Sadler dau.of Henry
12 Mar.1785,	Roger		Caty Quarles dau.of James, John Read sec.
10 Mar.1823,	Robert P.		Prudence Delbridge
28 Jan.1793,	Roland		Nancy Holiby, John Cheley sec.
27 Nov.1849,	Sterling		Martha E.Moore
24 Nov.1806,	Thomas		Frances Lanier
7 July 1813,	"		Eliz.M.Harrison
23 Dec.1811,	William		Rhoda Evans
2 Oct.1815,	"		Martha P.Harrison
21 Dec.1847,	"	P.	Eliz.Speake dau.of Martha
22 Nov.1819,	"	T.	Polly Williams
8 May 1798,	Wilson		Sally Allen, Robert Allen sec.
29 Nov.1790,	Zebulon		Nancy Anderton, Mordecai Howard sec.
26 Jan.1795, Williamson,	Charles		Polly Woolsey, Randolph Woolsey sec.
21 Oct.1758,	Jesse		Mary Parsons dau.of Thomas
21 Jan.1786,	John		Nancy Goodrich dau.of Briggs(W.B.V;278)
* * 1790s	Joseph,		Mason Allen, John Williamson sec.

14 July 1778, Williamson, Lewellin   to   Eliz.Clack

28 Apr.1772,   Stephen   Ann Collier, John Edmundson sec.

29 Apr.1771, Willis,   * * *   Eliz.Edwards dau.of Col.Nathaniel(IV;74)

14 Nov.1781,   Peter   Sarah Fowler   dau.of Daniel,(W.B.V;287)

17 Dec.1781, Willson,   Robert   Clara Fisher dau.of James, John Willson
                                                       sec.†

26 Nov.1823,   Thomas C.   Maria R.Gilliam

8 Dec.1797, Wilson,   Benjamih   Ann Lanier dau.of Winifred,Peter Wynne
                                                       sec.

25 Aug.1823,   Francis A.   Susan B.Gilliam

20 Mar.1820,   George   Eliza E.Brodnax

26 Nov.1787,   John   Eliz.Lester (O.B.XIV;206)

15 Jan.1801,   "   Ruth Ramsay

19 Dec.1827,   Legrand W.   Clara A.Aldridge

3 Apr.1778,   * *   Rebecca Stainback dau.of Francis(W.B.V;
                                                       57)

4 Mar.1726,   Thomas   Amy Urvin sau.of Eliz.Vol.1;266)

7 Oct.1801, Windham,   Kinchin   Eliz.Barnes dau.of Stephen

4 Nov.1777, Wingfield,   Joshua   Rebecca Carloss widow

12 Feb.1814,   Thomas   Martha Murrell

21 Jan.1786,   * *   Rebecca Thrower dau.of Hezekiah(W.B.V;
                                                       213)

4 Feb.1837, Winn,   Edmund   Nancy Oliver

18 Sept.1811,   Joseph   Clara Hammond dau.of William

10 Dec.1831,   Washington H. Harriet D.Maclin

19 Aug.1760, Wise,   * *   Mary Massie dau.of Joseph(W.B.III;370)

22 Feb.1773, Withers,   James   Judith Brown widow,John Powell sec.

28 May 1817,   William   Eliza Stith, Richard Stith sec.

12 Dec.1833, Wolff,   William B.   Ann E.Shell

133

7 May 1741, Wood,   Richard   to Mary Humphries exx.of John.(O.B.1;440)

1 Dec.1779, Woodard,   * *   Allis Hill dau.of John (W.B.V;98)

27 July 1801,   Edward   Jenny Spilman

24 Dec.1787, Woodleif,   George,   Katherine Clayton, Thomas Claiborne sec.

2 Apr.1747,   John   Catherine House exx.of Thomas Jr.(O.B.
                                                                   III;169)

22 Dec.1779, Woodroof,   Nathaniel   Catey Vick dau.of John, Howell Vick sec.

30 Apr.1840, Woodruff,   Benjamin D.   Susan Taylor dau.of Edward

28 Mar.1808,   George B.   Sally Manning

7 Feb.1839,   John   Pamela Braswell dau.of Jesse

19 July 1841,   Parsons   Eliz. L.Moss dau.of Meredith

28 Oct.1799, Woodson,   Peter   Betty Hobbs

23 Nov.1795, Woolsey   Abner   * *   * *   , Joseph Phipps sec.

23 Nov.1801,   John Moore   Nancy P.Smith

19 Sept.1827,Womack,   John P.   Louisa Ann Stith

5 June 1746,   William   Juliana Harris wid.of Francis,(O.B.III;
                                                                   37)

23 Oct.1804, Woodward,   Edmund   Rebecca Jordan

15 Nov.1803,   Owen   Keziah Wallace

1 Nov.1802, Woolsey,   * *   Eliz.Wheeler dau.of Benjamin,(W.B.VI;
                                                                   513)

25 July 1774,Worsham,   Lewellin   Eliz.Pettway, Edward Pettway sec.

24 Feb.1785,   Thomas   Betty Wynne, John Read sec.

5 Apr.1844, Wortham,   Richard   Ann R.Britt

15 July 1833,Worthington, Henry H.   Frances Crighton

30 Dec.1797,   Samuel   Martha Greenhill

17 June 1794,   William G.   Margaret M.Crichton dau.of James

20 Jan.1818, Wray,	Anderson,	to	Nancy Gibbs
8 Apr.1789,	Braxton		Mourning Jarrott, John Wray sec.
9 Aug.1847,	Douglas H.		Ann E.Moore
15 Jan.1844,	George W.		Frances E.Buckley
28 Dec.1841,	Henry		Jane McKenny dau.of Stacia
2 Jan.1801,	John		Patsey Brewer dau.of James
* * 1819,	"		Eliz.J.Wilkes
25 Sept.1843,	" B.		Mary Nolley
17 Feb.1848,	" W.		Jane Kirkland
23 Feb.1818,	Reuben		Sally Wesson
4 Apr.1848,	Samuel		Armantena Wright dau.of Lewis L.
25 Feb.1811,	Thomas		Lucy Richardson
27 Aug.1792,	Turner		Nancy Wray, Henry Wesson sec.
31 Mar.1826, Wrenn,	Benjamin J.		Rebecca A.Bailey
* Nov.1747,	John		Ann Carroll admx.of Thomas.(O.B.VII;34)
10 Nov.1829, Wright,	James s.of Letty,		Louisa Moore, dau.of Nancy
22 Nov.1831,	James S.		Jane E.Jones
28 Nov.1791,	Jarrot		Tabitha Howell, James Randall sec.
12 Oct.1796,	John		Polly Brewer, Willis Brewer sec.
20 Dec.1826,	" H.		Santhy C.Steed dau.of Jeduthen
27 Sept.1836,	" N.		Eliza Smith
25 Nov.1808,	Josias		Sally Wright
17 Jan.1809,	Merritt		Nancy Owens
3 Jan.1795,	Samuel		Sally Owen, George Wright sec.
27 Nov.1809,	Wesley		Creesy Birdsong
20 Dec.1810,	"		Mary M.Person

9 Jan.1843, Wright,	William G.to	Ann Smith
16 Feb.1773,	* * *	Eliz.Brown dau.of Richard (W.B.IV;148)
1 June 1826, Wyche,	Bevil G.	Lucy G.Edmunds
24 Aug.1826,	Henry	Margaret Warwick
11 Jan.1836,	Ira E.	A.C.Powell
9 Jan.1755,	James of Sux.	Leah Maclin, Nicholas Edmunds sec.
28 Mar.1774,	John	Priscilla Adams dau.of William,(OB.XII; 514)
3 Sept.1802,	"	Polly Hobbs dau.of Hubbard
3 Apr.1833,	"	Martha E.Astrop
26 May.1836,	Joseph	Margaret A.E.Harris, dau.of Robert
24 Jan.1790,	Nathaniel	Middleton Fletcher, James Fletcher sec.
14 Sept.1782,	Peter	Patty Harrison dau.of Benjamin,
23 Dec.1771,	William	* * Sims dau.of Adam (O.B.XI;430)
16 Aug.1760,	* *	Frances Brewer dau.of George,(W.B.III; 344)
9 Oct.1773,	* *	Patience Clark dau.of George(W.B.IV;448)
22 July 1844, Wynne,	Freeman J.	Ann E.Carrington
13 Jan.1783,	Gillamus	Rebecca Lester daul of Andrew
7 Dec.1824,	James	Nancy Cole
23 Nov.1772,	John	Mary Lyall, Joseph Lyall sec.
25 Oct.1790,	"	Mary Ingram 21 yrs., Jesse Penn sec.
16 Feb.1802,	"	Citivia Malone
27 Sept.1808,	"	Charlotte Edwards
6 Sept.1828,	"	Rebecca Goodwin
20 Jan.1802,	Lewellin	Eliz.Freeman
28 July 1823,	Parks	Julia Morris
8 Dec.1797,	Peter	Winifred Wilson dau.of John, Benjamin sec.

9 Aug.1750,	Wynne,	Robert	to Mary Phillipson widow.
9 Aug.1753,		"	Mary Johnson widow, Lawrence Gibbons sec.
25 Mar.1767,		"	Lucy Bobbett admx.of Thomas,(O.B.X;269)
16 Mar.1808,		William	Polly Wynne
15 Mar.1810,	Yates,	Benjamin P.	Eliz.F.Stith dau.of Griffin, Wm.Yates sec
7 Jan.1765,	Yeargins,	Thomas	Patty Burrow ? , Miles House sec.
14 Feb.1792,		William	Eliz.Rainey, Thomas Jones sec.
29 Jan.1796,	Yeargin,	Williams	Rebecca Bennet, John Bennet sec.
2 Apr.1825,	Young,	Edward	Elvira Connelly,
7 June 1822,		Joshua	Elvira Woodlief dau.of Eliz.
26 May 1783,		Mathew	* * admx.of Andrew Cubbin(O.B.XIII;145)
24 Sept.1794,		Samuel Jr.	Eliz.Love dau.of Fanny, Willie Harrison sec.
12 Feb.1835,		William	Susan Hawkins dau.of Edward (?)
30 Oct.1823,	Zachary,	Benjamin	Martha Mayton
27 Nov.1752,	Zell	John	Agness Peebles dau.of Henry (D.B.V;385)
22 Aug.1836,	Zemmer,	" L.	Mary Jane Short

OMISSIONS:

27 Feb.1785,	Pearson	* *	Patty Johnson dau.of John(W.B.V;154)
28 Feb.1799,		William	Ann Floyd
10 Jule 1820,		"	Nancy King
15 Nov.1803,	Randolph	Edward	Margaret S.Turnbull
10 Dec.1795,	Rhea,	Andrew	Susanna Stith dau.of Thomas Sr.
28 June 1799,	Rhodes,	Randolph	Pheobe Maddox
* *	1787-8,Randolph,	Harrison	Mary Jones
12 May 1778,		William	Mary Sims dau.of John)W.B.V;14)

A few marriage bonds copied from Southampton County:

* * Nov.1819, Claiborne, Gregory   to   Mary E.Weldon by Rev.Benj.Devanney.

11 Apr.1826,   Dr.James   Jane J.Weldon 21 yrs.,con.Samuel Blunt.

 9 Mar.1824, Field,   Theophilus   Louisa R.Ridley

17 Oct.1769, Edmunds, John Flood   Lucy Gray dau.of Joseph

12 Oct.1758, McLin,   Frederick   Priscilla Clements dau.of Benjamin

12 June 1760,   "   "   Lucy Rawlings spinster,Peter Butts scec.

15 Feb.1830, Maclin,   John D.   Louisa R.Field

30 Sept.1772, Pelham,   Peter Jr.   Parthenia Brown, John Atkinson's con.

 4 Nov.1850, Mallory, James B.   Mary Jane Drewry ward of Samuel Drewry

22 Aug.1764, Peete,   Thomas   Judith Clements dau.of Benjamin.

15 Dec.1762, Peterson, Batte   Mary Taylor sister of William

18 May 1846, Short,   Richard T.   Mary E.Jones ward of John F.Maclin.

12 Dec.1764, Stewart, Richard   Ann Myrick dau.of John & Ann.

11 Aug.1806, Stith,   Griffin   Margaret Bouthn Jones dau.of A.Jones

12 Feb.1753, Tazewell Littleton   Mary Gray spinster, Benj.Ruffin sec.

 6 Dec.1767, Turner,   Simon   Ann Williamson, William Williamson sec.

24 Mar.1763, Warren,   Benjamin   Rachel Washington, John Warren bec.

                    * * * * *

13 Jan.1774, Tazewell ,Henry of Brun.Dolly Waller dau.of Benjamin of William-
                                     Va.Gazette 13 Jan.1774.   sburg.

                    * * * * * *

Sussex County:

18 Aug.1777, Jones,   Mordecai   Eliz.Barnes widow, John Cargill wit.

21 Aug.1764, Peterson, John,of Brun. Eliz.Briggs,dau.of George

14 Feb.1769, Sisson,   Thomas   "   Martha Parker dau.of William decd.

-A-

Abernathy,_____ 68
  Abby 106
  Alice 62
  Amanda A. E. 70
  Blanche 4
  Catherine 71
  Clary 81
  Eliz. 95, 107, 126
  Jane 28
  Jane T. 121
  Lucy 11
  Martha 15, 104, 105
  Martha Ann 71
  Mary 4
  Mason 62
  Nancy 104
  Polly 102
  Rebecca 29, 59
  Silvey 69
  Susan 24
Adams,_____ 33
  Ann 50, 128
  Mary 31
  Polly 107
  Priscilla 135
  Prudence 109
  Sarah 7, 22, 68
Adkins, Patsy 79
  Rebecca 25
  Sarah 6
Aldridge, Clara A. 132
  Rebecca 11
Alexander, Martha 90
Allen, Betsey 9
  Eliz. 44
  Eliz. B. 93
  Eliza G. 19
  Mason 131
  Minerva M. 79
  Nancy 58, 69
  Sally 121, 128, 131
  Sarah 97
  Susan R. 29
Alley, Lucy 24
  Tabitha G. 40
Allgood, Ann 83
Anderson, Mary F. 103
Anderton, Eliz. 45
  Jane 45
  Nancy 131
Andrews, Hannah 6
  Maria M. 35
  Sarah 96
Archer, Sally H. 8
Astrop, Martha E. 135
Atkerson, Susan 111

Atkins, Aylce 115
  Catherine 112
  Mary A. B. 13
  Sarah 41, 74
  Susan 39
Atkinson, Dorothy 23
  Frances P. 55
  Lucy Y. 91
  Martha L. 47
  Mary 52
  Patsy 24
  Rebecca 19
  Susan W. 11
Avenhunt, Frances 110
Avent, Betsey 38
  Mourning 94
Avery, Eliz. 57
  Martha T. 1
  Pheobe 103
  Polly 67
  Sally 15
  Susanna 54

-B-

Bacon, Eliza A. 82
  Narcissa M. 127
Bagwell, Frances 101
  Keziah 111
  Susanna 96
Bailey,_____ 90
  Faith 57
  Holly 113
  Mary 19
  Patsey 107
  Rebecca A. 134
Baird, Amy 95
Baley, Eliz. 38
Ballentine, Eliz. 129
Banks, Eliz. L. 75
Barker, Eliz. 7
  Eliz. E. 112
  Eliz. G. 12
  Nancy 128
  Polly 20
  Sarah 106
Barner, Ann 18
  Eliz. 53, 103
  Eliz. P. 68
  Lucy 75
  Rebecca 52
Barnes, Clarissa Ann 97
  Eliz. 45, 132, 137
  Evelina 11
  Louisa 10
  Martha 34

Barnes (cont.)
  Mary A. 5
  Nancy 103
  Naomi 37
  Rebecca A. 37
  Susan K. 34
  Sylvia 95
  Tabitha A. 87
  Vicky 100
Barnner, Judith 92
Barrow, Anne 22
  Catherine 30
  Eliz. 23
  Jane 58
  Jean 3
  Margaret A. 73
  Mary 43, 53
  Mary F. A. 89
  Milly 27
  Mourning 9
  Nancy 31
  Polly 27
  Sally 114
  Sarah J. 24
Bartholomew, Eliz. 31
Baskerville, Mary 9
Bass, Ann 9
  Betsey 41, 130
  Darcus 1
  Eliz. 4, 42, 47
  Eliz. H. 52
  Eliz. S. 67
  Lucy 80, 111
  Martha 13
  Martha M. 105
  Mary 34
  Mary A. E. 2
  Nancy 71, 111
  Polly 121
  Rebecca 14, 108
  Rebecca H. 10
  Silvia 50
  Tempe(y) 124
Batte, Catherine 58
  Martha 47
  Tabitha H. 29
Baugh, Eliz. B. 91
  Mary G. 15
  Nancy 48
  Nancy W. 91
  Sarah 10
  Susanna 7
  Tabitha 74
Beard, Charlotte 86
Beasley, Mary A. 128
  Rebecca J. 80
Beck, Eliz. 83
  Rebecca 32
Bennet, Nancy 54

Bennet (cont.)
  Rebecca 136
Bennett, Agness E. 64
  Eliz. 47
  Judith 8
Bentley, Amanda A. 59
Berry, Eliz. 25
  Molly 25
  Patsey 121
  Polly 25
Berryman, Lucy 66
Bethshares, Nancy 54
Betty, Charlotte 68
  Eliz. 90
  Frances 75
  Martha 7
  Mary 9
  Nancy 130
  Polly 87
Biggs, Betsy 46
  Lucy 31
  Mary Ann C. 79
  Sally 79
  Susan 79
Birchett, Agness 123
  Becky 80
  Patty 29
  Polly 78, 86
Birdsong, Becke 63
  Creecy/Creesy 2, 134
  E. 131
  Judith C. 46
  Mary 51
  Mary A. 104
  Nancy 16
  Rebecca 108, 129
  Sarah 102
Birthright, Ann W. 119
  Eliz. 48
Bishop, Angelica 22
  Catherine R. 117
  Lucretia 16, 73
  Lucy S. 114
  Martha 36, 85
  Martha M. 104
  Martha R. 43
  Matthew J. 91
  Mary 80
  Rebecca 125
  Sally J. 79
  Susan A. E. 104
Bithshurs, Tabitha 83
Blake, Ellen W. 11
Blanch, Luch K. 30
  Nancy T. 130
  Rebecca 125
  Sarah W. 75
Blank, Nancy 23
Blankenship, Levinia 41
Blick,_____100
  Ann E. C. 118
  Mary Ann J. 4
  Sarah Ann 66
Blunt, M. Argyra 128
  Polly 5
Bobbett, Lucy 136
Bolling, Mildred M. 110
Bonner, Mary E. 78
  Minerva W. 64
Booth, Ann 54
  Flavia 24
  Harriet S. 68
  Margaret 6
  Mary 55
Boram, Frances A. 77
Boswell, Catherine 51
  Eliz. 27, 51
  Susan 111

Bott, Eliza L. 12
  Lucy M. 64
  Virginia Ann 63
Bottom, Eliza L. 35
  Natsy 63
  Sally L. 37
Bottow, Mary Ann P. 24
Bowen, Caroline R. 58
Bracey, Frances Eliz. 54
  Tabitha 63
Bradley, Martha A. 2
  Mary 58
  Polly 57
Bran, Ann 34
Branch, Rebecca A. 41
Branders, Lucy 56
Brann, Caty 35
Brantley, Luch S. 91
Braswell, Ann P. 80
  Betsy 115
  Nancy 130
  Pamela 133
  Sally 37
  Tabitha 81
Braton, Rebecca 35
Brent, Margaret 13
Brett, Rebecca 57
Brewer, Dorothy 13
  Frances 135
  Lucy 2
  Lurana 87
  Middleton 23
  Nancy 89
  Patsey 134
  Polly 134
  Rachel 18
  Rebecca 18
  Sally 89
  Sarah 122
  Winifred 18
Bridgforth, Eliz. 5, 61
  Maria 42
  Susan 25
Briggs, Eliz. 64, 137
  Martha 26
  Mary 90
  Rebecca 114
Brigs, Lucrecy 94
Britt, Ann R. 133
  Jane C. 75
  Lucy 124
  Martha 89
  Mary 124
  Milly 23
Britton, Mary A. 125
Brittle, Rainey 52
Broadus, Sally 62
Brock, Martha J. 2
Brodnax,_____94, 123
  Ann 36, 48, 128
  Eliz. 35
  Eliza E. 132
  Emily H. 71
  Martha K. 51
  Mary 109
  Rebecca 53
Browder, Betsey 44
  Biddy 129
  Catherine 85
  Erman 63
  Loise 20
  Mary 6
  Mary Kelly 71
  Mary W. 103
  Nancy R. 85
  Sally 5
  Susanna 23
Brown, Agnes P. M. J. 62

Brown (cont.)
  Amanda 53
  Armon 26
  Betty 5, 24
  Edna 114
  Eliz. 97, 100, 135
  Frances 16, 128
  Francis 82
  Joany 51
  Judith 132
  Loisa 104
  Lucy D. 42
  Martha 38, 75
  Martha F. 119
  Mary 105, 123
  Mary Ann 95
  Mary S. 118
  Nancy 30, 79
  Parthenia 137
  Polly 94, 98
  Sarah 27
  Suckey 17
Bruce, Hannah 121
  Polly 27
Bryan, Lucretia 60
Bsandus [?], Polly 18
Buchana, Patsey 36
Buckley, Frances E. 134
  Harriet 37
  Luch Ann 52
Buckner, Eliz. 8, 81, 109
  Eliz. J. W. 115
  Judith 60
  Nanch C. 79
Buford, Mary A. C. 101
Burch, Eliz. 25, 67
  Jenny 118
  Martha 29
  Mary 76
  Nancy 108
Burge, Ann 70
  Martha 23, 95
  Polly 2, 61
  Prissy 117
  Sarah 3, 99
  Temperence 116
Burks, Eliz. R. 65
  Milly 104
  Polly 109
Burnett, Ann F. 16
  Eliz. 120
Burrow, Frances 127
Burrow(?), Patty 136
Burton, Sarah J. 72
Butler, Rebecca 125
Butterill, Eliz. 61
Butts, Eliz. A. 100
  Sarah 107

-C-

Callis, Mary E. 62
Cammell, Lucy 28
Camp, Mary 40
Campbell, Tabitha 7
Cannon, Biddy 13
Capel, Frances 37
Capell, Sally 109
Cargill, Lucy Binns 60
  Sarah H. 76
Carloss, Rebecca 132
Carpenter, Eliz. 127
  Julia Ann 17
  Nancy 115
Carrington, Ann E. 135

Carrington (cont.)
  Martha S. 56
  Rebecca B. 29
Carroll, Ann 134
Carter, Catherine 3
  Lucy 74
Cary, Nancy 112
Cashon, Harriet 101
Cattles, Nancy 96
Caudle, Rebecca 28
Cauze, Ann 101
Ceely, Martha 96
  Mary 63
Chamberlayne, Eliz. 67
Chambliss, Diana J. 20
  Molly 38
  Rebecca 99
Chapman, Ann 40
  Emeline S. 84
  Isabella 58
  Mary J. C. 49
  Rebecca 123
  Rebecca W. 115
Charles, Lucy 91
  Mary 111
Cheely, Ann 10
  Dolly W. 38
  Eliz. 23
  Julia 57
  Julia H. 70
  Maria L. 23
  Martha 113
  Mary F. 20
  Polly 37
  Priscilla 42
  Susan 82
  Winifred F. 71
Childress, Sarah 100
Christie, Keziah 46
Clack, Agness Bolling 61
  Ann 92
  Betty 2
  Dolly 72
  Dorothy 9
  Eliz. 120, 132
  Eliza P. 101
  Mary 101
  Sally 73
Claiborne, Adelaide H.E. 94
  Ann Barbar 41
  Anna M. 17
  Augusta 116
  Martha J. 21
  Mary 29
  Nancy S. 39
Clanton, Ann 59
  Sarah 66
Clark, Amey 85
  Ann 15
  Eliz. 79, 90, 130
  Mary 7, 24, 90
  Patience 135
  Susanna 112
  Wilmouth 85
Clarke, Eliz. 129
  Eliz. D. 27
  Eveline G. 78
  Mary 90, 115
  Polly 53
  Prudence 25
  Temperence 113
Clary,_____ 51, 89
  Jane A. 71
  Lucy 74
  Nancy 126
Clary(?), Judith 61
Clayton, Anneliza 30

Clayton (cont.)
  Catherine 3
  Eliz. Seward 50
  Katherine 133
  Lucy 64
  Marietta A. 1
  Martha 82
  Rebecca 84
  Sally 20
Cleary, Patty 10
Clegg, Susan 71
Clements, Judith 137
  Patty 28
  Priscilla 137
Clemons, Jean 69
Cocke, Ann 20
  Betty 70
  Eliz. 56
  Fanny 86
  Mary 75
  Susanna 23
Cole, Ann J. 113
  Jane 127
  Levinia 123
  Nancy 135
  Sally 52
Coleman, Dorothy 90
  Juliette 113
  Mary A. H. 21
  Mary Ann 117
Coley, Eliz. 50
  Mary Ann 86
Collier, Ann 40, 80, 87, 132
  Betsy 114
  Betty 72
  Eliz. 4, 31, 50, 70, 110
  Eliz. G. 25
  Faithy 80
  Frances 27
  Hannah 42
  Judith 54
  Lucy R. 13
  Martha 8
  Martha H. 120
  Mary L. 5
  Nancy 45
  Nancy S. 77
  Polly 79
  Rebecca 9
  Sarah 50
  Sarah V. 2
  Susanna 113
  Tabitha J. 42
Collins, Huldy 26
  Jane T. 79
Conneley, Martha 119
  Subina 90
Connell, Catherine 48
  Eliz. 77
Connelley, Hannah 40
Connelly, Eliza H. 6
  Elvira 136
  Martha H. 5
Constable, Jane 62
Cook/Cooke, Anne 70
  Betty 90
  Eliz. 23
  Flora 112
  Jane 19
  Mary 67
  Milly 10
  Molly 128
  Patsy 79
  Polly 114
  Rebecca 14, 51
  Sally 85

Cook/Cooke (cont.)
  Sarah 10, 99
Cooksey, Mary 104
Cordle, Ann 99
  Sally 27
  Sarah 65
  Susanna 129
Courtney, Ann 72
Cousins, Frances R. 61
Crichton, Margaret M. 133
Crighton, Frances 133
  Martha J. 120
  Rose A. 69
Crittenden, Frances 41
  Susan 48
Croft, Eliz. 58
  Nancy W. 1
Crook, Caty 118
  Eliz. 66
  Mary 8
  Polly 43, 105
Cross, Catherine 76
Crowder, Eliz. 30
  Nancy 36
  Polly 119
Cryer, Anne 73
Cumming, Mary Eliza 119
Curtis, Kezia 91
  Lucy 74

-D-

Dailey, Eliz. 74, 81
  Frances 130
  Sarah 12
Dameron, Angelica F. 14
  Ann Morehead 6, 77
  Martha C. 106
  Mary 59
  Sarah 62
Dance, Nancy 37, 85
  Sally 95
  Sarah 40
Daniel, Anana 15
  Ann 17, 93
  Diana 6
  Elinor B. 96
  Eliz. 93
  Eliz. A. 96
  Eliza Ann 6
  Ermine 6
  Frances 28
  Jane 23, 96
  Martha 42
  Mary 53, 88
  Mary Ann 2
  Sarah 32
  Susanna 93
Davenport, Eliz. 1
  Frances 86
  Jincy 111
  Milly 1
  Polly W. 130
Davis, Bridgett 46
  Eliz. 15, 16, 102
  Eliz. D. 47
  Eliza J. 22
  Eliza M. 22
  Jane A. 11
  Lucinda F. 55
  Martha 7, 37, 74, 85
  Mary 108
  Mary M. 54
  Nancy 35
  Polly 105

Davis (cont.)
  Rejoice 31
  Sarah G. 102
  Susan 96
Dawson, Mary 17
  Priscilla 60
Davy, Rebecca Ann 117
Day, Lucy 27
  Susanna 89
Dean, Sally 88
  Susanna 88
Delbridge,_____ 126
  Eliz. 51, 89, 125
  Harietta C. 108
  Jane K. B. 129
  Martha 79
  Mary J. 89
  Nancy 126
  Polly 68
  Priscilla M. 61
  Prudence 131
  Rebecca Ann 21
  Sally 57
  Sarah E. 68
  Virginia A. C. A.? 51
Deloach, Anne 55
  Celia 92
  Martha 55
Denton,_____ 70
  Pamelia 123
Dixon, Ann R. 50
  Betsey 93
  Clara A. 16
  Eliza 1
  Nancy 113
  Sally 113
Dobbins, Polly 69
Doby, Eliz. 39
  Mary 29
Doley, Sarah 26
Donaldson, Ann 55
  Eliz. 120
  Hannah 99
  Sarah 55
Douglas, Eliz. 49
  Susan 73
  Susanna 73
Douglass, Frances S. 19
Downing, Eliz. 54
Doyal, Sally 48
Doyle, Rebecca J. 64
Drake, Mary T. 84
  Rebecca 121
Drewry, Mary Jane 137
Driscoll, Sarah A. 91
Dromgoole, Eliz. 45
  Fanny H. 86
  Isabella 101
  Louisa 110
  Mary C. 107
  Rebecca 51, 107
Drummond, Ann E. 28
  Margaret 44
  Margaret C. 112
  Maria E. 44
Duane, Eliz. E. 119
Duggar, Ammond 64
  Ann B. 64
  Eliz. 111
  Eliz. F. 130
  Fanny 15, 97
  Frances 95
  Harriet A. 48
  Louisa 111
  Lucretia 3
  Luvany 94
  Margaret 117
  Mary 31

Duggar (cont.)
  Nancy 82
  Nancy B. 10
  Polly 69, 121
  Rebecca L. 103
  Sally 73, 74
  Sally H. 75
  Sarah 97
  Susan H. 80
  Susanna 99
Dugger, Armon 30
  Sally 30
Dunkley, Eliz. 116
  Frances 69
  Martha 67
  Mary A. M. 99
  Susan J. 6
Dunman, Amy 4
Dunn, Betty 94
  Frances 104
  Francis Jane 35
  Molly 131
Dunnington, Eliz. 47
Dunnivant, Martha C. 110
Dupree, Eliz. Donaldson
  117
DuPriest, Minerva 125
Durham, Clarissa 2
  Margaret 56

        -E-

Eanes, Tabitha 66
Easter, Mary 2
Eaves, Ann 41
  Eliz. 99
Edmunds,_____ 94
  Ann 125
  Charlotte 73
  Clarissa 98
  Eliz. 38, 68
  Harriet 20, 94
  Julia 73
  Lucy G. 135
  Mary 70
  Middy 21
  Rahab 62
  Sally 36
  Sally Ann 96
  Sara 103
  Sarah 105
  Susan 53
  Susanna 73
Edmundson, Sarah 103
Edwards,_____ 88
  Brambley 64
  Charity 96
  Charlotte 135
  Dianah 129
  Dolly 82
  Eleanor H. 16
  Eliz. 82, 132
  Eliz. P. 74
  Jane W. 127
  Julia E. 111
  Martha 48, 111
  Mary 2, 3, 8, 100
  Nancy 30
  Obedience 94
  Permely 95
  Polly 66, 81
  Rebecca 2, 59, 125
  Ruth 123
  Sarah 81, 97
  Susanna 87

Edwards (cont.)
  Tabitha 121
  Tempe 52
  Temperence 4
Elder, Nancy 9
  Phebe 26
Eldride, Mary Ann 81
Eldridge, Emmeline T. 49
  Martha 61
  Nancy 123
  Paulene 31
  Sarah 32
  Sarah R. 21
Elliott, Martha M. 72
  Mary 122
  Nancy W. 11
  Sarah 122
Elmore, Eliz. 113
  Nancy 114, 115
  Polly 96
  Sally 14
  Sarah 18
  Susan 27
Elzey, Eliz. 2
Embrey, Martha 107
Embry, Martha 34
  Mary 78
  Priscilla 55
Emmery, Tempy 121
Epes, Martha Ann 59
Epperson, Martha 113
  Martha A. 59
  Sally 102
  Sally Ann 121
Eppes, Susanna 77
Evans, Eliz. 70, 130
  Rhoda 131
  Susanna 59
Ezell, Dolly W. 104
  Eliz. 87
  Eliz. A. 81
  Eliz. C. 105
  Jane 56, 105
  Polly D. 35
  Sally 111
  Susanna 18, 35

        -F-

Fann, Lucretia 118
Farler, Eliz. 65
Farlow, Roanna M. 128
Fearson, Charlotte 40
  Faithy 40
Fenn, Arian F. 71
Ferguson, Nancy 113
  Rebecca 23
  Rebecca F. 2
  Sally 24
Field, Ann E. 34
  Ann M. 47
  Henrietta M. 72
  Louisa R. 137
  Lucy G. 129
  Margaret B. 77
  Martha R. 119
  Sally Ann 8
  Susan E. 66
Finch, Mary 80
  Polly 37
  Rebecca 9
Firth, Betsy 97
  Eliz. 98
  Polly 16
  Polly B. 30

Firth (cont.)
 Rebecca 1
 Sally 95
Fisher, Clara 132
 Constance 95
 Eliz. 40
 Martha 33
 Polly 49
 Sarah 26
 Susan J. H. 32
Fletcher, Lucy C. B. 37
 Martha E. 7
 Middleton 135
 Nancy A. 80
 Rebecca 65
 Rebecca J. 7
 Sally 7
 Sarah 84
 Sarah E. W. 91
Floyd, _____ 54
 Amy 82
 Ann 136
 Eliz. 77, 92
 Eliz. J. 37
 Maria S. 103
 Martha 82, 107
 Martha A. 126
 Mary 12
 Mary Jane 43
 Nancy 125
 Patsey 90
 Pheobe 27
 Sally 37
Foart, Marian 53
Fort, Eliz. 100
 Lucy 109
 Martha 108
 Sally 24
Foster, Betsy 117
 Dolly 41
 Herison 107
 Lucy C. 18
 Sally B. 27
 Susanna 81
Fowler, Mary 130
 Sarah 132
Fowlkes, Eliz. 89
 Lucy 118
 Polly G. 43
 Poly Jennings 43
Fox, Lucy 101
 Mary 59
 Winifred 101
Frayser, Martha 124
Freeman, Agness 123
 Eliz. 94, 135
 Keziah 78
 Lucy 127
 Polly 57
 Frisbie, Sarah A. 98

-G-

Gargus, Nancy 109
Garris, Lydia 71
Garrott, Susanna 121
Gee, Betsy 45
 Bridgett 28
 Eliz. 50
 Eliz. R. 4
 Eliza 51
 Emry B. 116
 Hannah 93
 Lucy W. 78
 Margaret S. 48

Gee (cont.)
 Martha A. E. 48
 Mary 24
 Mary Jane 90
 Nancy 23
 Parthenia 87
 Penelope 93
 Priscilla 27
 Rebecca 103
 Sally 126
 Susan 102
 Susanna 100
George, Lucy 107
Gholson, Anne E. 55
 Eliz. 38
 Martha 52
 Nancy 93
Gibbon, Lucy J. 65
Gibbs, Delitha 113
Gibbs, Eliz. 104
 Nancy 134
 Patsy 63
 Sarah 67
Gilliam, Ann 11
 Eliz. 87
 Eliza Yates 63
 Louisa S. 103
 Maria R. 132
 Roberta C. 12
 Selah D. 22
 Susan B. 132
Gladish, Betsey 50
 Martha 13
Goode, Jane 11
Goodrich, Eliz. B. 40
 Frances Eliz. 14
 Lucy 41
 Molly 13
 Nancy 131
 Nancy Kemp 49
 Rebecca 19
 Sally 12
 Sarah 117
Goodrum, Polly 58
Goodwin, Rebecca 135
Goodwyn, Eliza 32
 Helen L. 112
 Maria Louisa 68
Gordon, Nancy M. 113
Grammer, Ann 34
Granger, Polly 64
Gray, Lucy 137
 Mary 137
Green, Ann 99
 Eliz. 74
 Eliz. B. 102
 Frances E. 124
 Jane 90
 Lucy 40
 Martha Cary 80
 Mary P. 41
 Patty 47
 Sally G. 49
 Sarah 126
Greene, Mary 40
Greenhill, Catherine C. 58
 Martha 25, 133
Gregg, Martha Jane 25
 Susan W. 129
Gregory, Oney 83
Gresham, Christiana 125
 Mary 46
 Patty 5
 Tabitha 71
Griffin, Amaza 5
 Martha J. 130
 Mary W. 121

Griffin (cont.)
 Sarah E. 60
Griffith, Nancy 84
Griffiths, Nancy 83
Grigg, Mary W. 12
 Patty 10
 Sarah E. 87
Grimes, Martha 22
Grubbs, Eliz. 96
 Susanna 98
Gunn, Milly 5
 Nancy 83
 Sarah 46
 Susanna 128

-H-

Hackley, Harriet R. 82
Hagood, Eliz. 7, 23, 77, 130
 Mary 19
 Rebecca Ann 7
Hailey, Caty 42
Haley, Dolly 99
Hall, Lucy 54, 124
 Martha 19
 Polly 8
 Rebecca 2
 Sally 126
 Sarah 25, 50
Hamblett, Ann 92
 Susanna 36
Hamilton, Susanna 72
Hamlet, Writter 78
Hammond, Betsy L. 58
 Clara 132
 Nancy 6
Hammons, Mary 27
Hamour, Tabitha 44
Hampton, Eliz. 85
 Emily 34
 Jean 55
 Louisa 109
 Nancy 81
Hancock, Anthanico 51
 Dorothy 51
 Eliz. 33
 Patsy 57
 Polly 76
Hanks, Mildred 78
Hanner, Martha E. 65
Hansell, Ann 72
Hardaway, Ann 20
 Eliz. 122
 Frances 17, 19, 26
 Martha 71
 Mary 21
 Mason 15
 Nancy 89
 Rebecca 83
 Sarah 111
Hardie, Eliz. 77
Hardy, Anne 22
Harmon, Rebecca 32
Harper, Mary 23
 Rebecca 89
Harris, Cetian 71
 Eliz. 84
 Eliz. P. 63
 Eliza D. 93
 Juliana 133
 Margaret A. E. 135
 Martha 108
 Martha A. G. 97
 Martha B. 107

143

Harris (cont.)
Mary C. 131
Matilda R. 32
Nancy 98
Patty 5
Polly 127
Priscilla 81
Sarah 22
Susan M. J. 31
Susanna 113
Harrison, Amanda E. O.
106
Ann 53, 54, 76
Anne 110, 123
Araminta 94
Argyra 11
Ariana R. 119
Chrictian 49
Dolly 110
Eliz. 5, 37, 50
Eliz. M. 131
Eliza R. 110
Fanny 3
Frances 70, 87
Frances F. 107
Hannah 98
Jane 130
Jenny 100
Lucy 70
Martha 11, 14, 65, 66
Martha A. 32
Martha L. 80
Martha P. 131
Mary 130
Mary B. 10
Mary E. 89
Mary W. 21
Minerva J. 39
Nancy 12, 19, 26, 45,
54, 67, 92, 125
Naomi 66
Olive 78, 110
Patty 135
Penelope H. 5
Polly 94, 110, 113
Rita 24
Rosalia E. 116
Sarah 65
Sarah Ann 65
Susan E. 57
Tabitha 12, 23, 25
Hartwell, Betsey 38
Emma A. C. 124
Evalina 99
Juliet 87
Louisa S. 124
Nancy 110
Polly 56
Sophronia 71
Harwell, Amy 91
Eliz. 15
Frances 66
Martha S. 106
Mary H. 44
Mary L. 4
Nancy 98
Nancy James 9
Patsy 41
Sarah 75, 100
Susanna 1, 114
Haskins, Eliz. C. 53
Lucy G. 112
Martha 32
Nancy 60
Sarah S. 17
Susan Edmunds 78
Hawkins, Clary Ann 39
Eliz. 17

Hawkins (cont.)
Elvy E. 46
Eveline G. 115
Frances Ann 65
Julia 35
Lucy C. 91
Mariah G. 129
Martha 67
Nancy C. 34
Quintina 116
Sarah S. 115
Susan 136
Hawks, Martha 27
Hawthorn, Mary A. 38
Rebecca 79
Susanna 53
Haygood (see Hagood)
Haymour, Jane 115
Hayne, Eliz. 125
Hearn, Ann 29
Eliz. 28
Martha 80
Mary 128
Heartwell, Antoinette C.
98
Louisa B. 46
Hickman, Lucy 83
Hicks, Catherine 122
Eliz. 44
Eliz. B. 11
Elizabeth 18
Frances 43, 97, 125
Frances A. 27
Hannah 21
Jean 91
Judith 23
Louisa G. 112
Lucretia 83
Lucy 105
Lucy W. 16
Martha 8
Mary 4
Minerva 17
Nancy V. 123
Polly 51
Rebecca 11, 117, 123
Rebecca B. 54
Sally 11, 53
Sarah 44
Susanna E. 124
Tabitha 12, 39, 57
High, Sally 118
Hightower, Hannah 120
Martha 31
Mary B. 118
Sarah 46
Hill, Allis 133
Ann D. 57
Eliz. 80
Eliz. W. 83
Frances W. B. 8
Hannah 88, 114
Minerva G. 34
Nancy 35
Nancy G. 13
Priscilla 130
Rebecca 114
Sarah 118
Temperence 22
Hinton, Ann E. J. 105
Mary W. 55
Hite, Henrietta A. 15
Hobbs, Betsey 35
Betty 133
Lucy 45
Martha 70
Polly 135
Sally 74

Hogan, Mary 65
Obedience 78
Hogwood, Sally 110
Holderby, Mary C. 116
Holiby, Nancy 131
Holloway, Eliza E. H. 123
Mary 29
Nellie 52
Quentena 60
Timma 12
Hood, Sarah 59
House, Ann E. 117
Catherine 95, 133
Eleanor 25
Eliz. 44
Frances 57
Jane 71
Martha 119, 123
Martha C. 45
Mary A. 30
Mary E. 105
Milly D. 84
Nancy 83, 126
Nancy N. 116
Polly 9
Sally V. 120
Tabitha 20, 130
Winifred 10
Howard, Eliz. 84
Hannah 127
Nancy 58
Howell, Eliz. L. 68
Louisa J. 59
Martha M. 50
Mary 91
Nancy F. 97
Tabitha 134
Howerton, Eliz. 28
Nancy 9
Sally 96
Howze, Frances 106
Hubbard, Emily J. 97
Lucy 69
Hudson, Dianotia P. 110
Jane B. 42
Parthenia 73
Tabitha J. C. 2
Huff, Eliz. 112
Milly 12
Molly Monk 14
Nancy 46
Olive 83
Rebecca 75
Santhy 102
Tabitha 46, 108
Hull, Fanny M. 123
Humphries, Mary 133
Hungerford, Ariana W. 109
Helen A. 110
Hunicutt, Ann L. 71
Hunnicutt, Caroline 109
Mary L. 112
Sally P. 47
Hunt, Ann 43
Sarah 17
Hunter, Eliz. 38
Hunwell, Martha 73
Huskey, Amey 98
Silvia 14
Hutchins, Polly 3
Hyde, Letitia 43

-I-

Ingram, Amey 12
  Ann 8
  Charlotte 89
  Eliz. 32, 42, 88, 112,
    121, 127
  Eliz. G. 127
  Eliz. H. 6
  Framcina 36
  Gracey 124
  Mary 49, 73, 135
  Mary Ann 47, 119
  Nancy 49
  Patty 21
  Polly 28
  Sally 33
  Sarah 29
  Susan 15
  Susanna 43
  Tabitha 39
Irby, Ann 101
  Anne 101
  Eliz. 113
Ivey, Patty 52
Ivie, Betsey R. 48
  Nancy Harrison 36
  Rebecca 40
  Sally B. 18

-J-

Jackson, _____ 52, 67
  Abigail 52
  Ann 53
  Anna 72, 83
  Anne 69
  Cornelia A. 128
  Eliz. 48, 97
  Eliza W. 89
  Fortune 78
  Hannah 5
  Jane 7, 55
  Judith S. 31
  Lucy 91
  Mary 118
  Mary F. 5
  Nancy 41, 92
  Patsy 24
  Polly 9, 129
  Rebecca 98, 125
  Rebecca Ann 14
  Sally 29
  Sandal 69
  Sarah 4, 25, 61
  Susanna 58
  Tabitha 107
  Temperence W. 14
James, Amanda R. 54
  Charlotte 112
  Eliz. 13
  Frances L. 2
  Martha 44
  Polly 123
  Rebecca 20
  Sally 38
  Sarah A. W. 94
Jameson, Mary 34
Jarrett, Patsey 8
Jarrott, Mary 39
  Mourning 134
Jenkins, Polly G. 5
Jennings, Francis M. 1

Jennings (cont.)
  Mary Jane 7
  Mary Jane Rebecca 24
Jessee, Eliz. 91
Jett, Martha F. 84
  Mary 128
  Nancy 18
Johnson, Amelia F. 27
  Ann 68
  Ann E. 1
  Betsy L. 15
  Eliz. 34, 70, 114, 126
  Ellen 104
  Fanny 14, 18
  Frances 105
  Frances E. 58
  Jane 40, 68
  Jincy 6
  Louisa S. 20
  Lucy 38, 123
  Mary 136
  Patty 136
  Polly G. 86
  Sally 59, 80, 123
  Sarah 6
  Sarah A. M. 59
  Tabitha 14
  Unity 76
Jolly, Eliz. 127
  Sarah E. 30
Jones, Abby 122
  Ann 16, 37, 77, 120
  Anna 61
  Betty 76
  Christiana B. 60
  Delila 66
  Dionasia 111
  Dolly 41
  Eliz. 10, 28, 78, 104,
    112, 126
  Eliz. B. 128
  Eliz. C. 16
  Eliza A. B. 47
  Frances 47
  Franky 102
  Hannah 73, 79
  Hannah B. 77
  Harriet J. 46
  Jane E. 134
  Jane W. 42
  Jinny 10
  Judy 69
  Louisa A. 59
  Lucy 73
  Lucy B. 76
  Lucy G. 122
  Margaret Bouth 137
  Martha 28, 92
  Martha D. 130
  Martha E. 7
  Martha F. 73
  Martha G. 105
  Mary 84, 94, 136
  Mary A. E. 88
  Mary E. 137
  Mary F. 42
  Minerva W. 31
  Molly 114
  Nancy 20, 31, 127
  Nancy E. C. 13
  Patty 51, 73
  Polly 73
  Prisey 81
  Rebecca 65
  Sally 69, 82, 87
  Sarah 14
  Sarah C. 76
  Susan Julia 18

Jones (cont.)
  Vespena E. 43
  Wilmouth 122
Jordan, Jane 78
  Mary 26, 99
  Rebecca 63, 133
  Sally 108
  Selah 34
Judd, Audney 60
  Eliz. W. 114
  Eliza S. 51
  Mary French 20
  Nancy 31
Justice, Betsy 127
  Franky 81
  Mary 83
  Polly 40
  Sarah 81
Justys, Patsy 18

-K-

Keats, Letitia 109
Keatt, Martha 60
Keatts, Caty 118
  Frances 60
  Mary B. 100
Keen, Eliz. 109
Kelley, Betsey 16
  Eliz. 45
  Sarah W. 25
Kelly, Amyusta S. 64
  Clerky 68
  Eliz. 43, 56, 71
  Elmira B. 68
  Louisa 21
  Lucy 127
  Margaret 76
  Mary 61
  Nancy 1, 5
  Rebecca 3
  Rhoda 76
  Susan 70
  Susan E. 97
  Winifred 21
Kemp, Ann 101
  Ezabel 19
Kennedy, Frances J. 6
  Jean 88
  Mary E. 53
Kidd, Ann C. 105
King, Amey 108
  Ann 110
  Ariana M. 71
  Dolly 119
  Eliz. 24
  Eliz.(?) 3
  Judith 69
  Julia Ann 93
  Lucy F. B. 105
  Martha 105
  Martha J. 112
  Mary 35, 57
  Molly 1
  Molly Betsey 35
  Nancy 68, 136
  Obedience 19
  Sarah 24, 80
  Sarah Ann 106
Kirk, Eliz. L. 108
  Nancy 11
Kirkland, Adeline 111
  Frances 16
  Frances E. 94
  Jane 134

145

Kirkland (cont.)
  Martha 32
  Martha C. W. 90
  Mary 8, 68
  Mary Ann 113
  S. A. J. 79
  Sally 16
  Susanna 95
  Tabitha 33

-L-

Laffoon, Eliz. 3, 80
  Lucretia 103
  Mary 85
Lafoon, Celia H. 47
Lambert, Ann 43
  Ann E. 64
  Eliz. 49
  Lorana 64
  Martha T. 65
  Mary S. 81
  Mildred 43
  Rebecca 77
Lane, Eliz. 2
  Judith 128
  Lucy 37
  Nancy 96
  Patsey 104
  Patsy 106
  Polly 87
  Susan 11
  Sylvia 50
Lanier,_____ 46
  Agness 28
  Ann 33, 132
  Betsy 56
  Catherine 11
  Eliz. 16, 91, 108
  Eliz. P. 46
  Frances 131
  Harriet S. 122
  Julia Ann 71
  Lucy 29
  Manerva 114
  Martha E. 44
  Mary 26, 100
  Mary Ann S. 10
  Molly 76
  Nancy 55, 106
  Patsey 6
  Polly 28, 87
  Sally 39, 126
  Sarah 5, 55
  Susan J. 9
  Winifred 129
Lashley, Julia 64
  Martha A. 100
  Polly 50
  Sally 93
Lattimore, Sarah E. 32,
  119
Laurence, Rebecca 77
  Sarah 102, 116
Lawler, Margaret 88
Lawrence, Ann 61
  Susan 9
Leadbetter, Sally 127
Ledbetter, Betsey 45
  Eliz. 129
  Mary 12, 41
  Polly 56
  Sarah 83
  Winifred 63
Lee, Clary H. 95

Lee (cont.)
  Susan 65
Lenoir, Eliz. 57
  Winifred 20
Lester, Eliz. 15, 132
  Hannah 120
  Mary 129
  Rachel 18
  Rebecca 135
  Sarah 78
Lett, Ann 109
  Polly 121
Lewis, Ann 68
  Ann E. 27
  Catherine 103
  Eliz. 64, 119
  Eliz. S. 55
  Louisa G. 128
  Lucy 129
  Lucy G. 55
  Maria 20
  Martha 20, 74, 86
  Mary 60
  Nancy 1
  Rhody 74
  Virginia M. 119
Lightfoot, Becky 26
  Celia 37
  Molly 103
  Patty 58
  Polly 49
  Rebecca 52
  Sally 60
Lilly, Ann C. 9
Linch, Nancy B. 54
  Rachel 69
  Vyny 98
Lindsay, Sarah 25
Little, Lucy 120
Livesey, Pheobe 110
Lockett, Ann C. 122
Loftin, Eliz. 52
Love, Eliz. 136
  Erminia E. 78
  Fanny 112
  Janet 125
  Katherine 30
  Mary 51
  Peggy 91
Loyd, Eliz. 48
  Nancy 95
Lucas, Eliz. W. 30
  Patsy 15
  Rebecca 95
  Rebecca R. 48
  Tabitha 90
Lucey, Patty 105
  Sally 107
Lucy, Amanda E. A. 103
  Eliz. 86
  Elizabeth 2
  Lavinia 91
  Levinia 96
  Maria 109
  Martha 104
  Sally 127
  Sally Ann 61
  Tabitha J. 126
Lundie, Ann J. S. 44
  Ann Jean 107
  Eliz. 3
  Susan 44, 98
Lundy, Ann D. 73
  Susan 98
Lyall, Mary 135
Lynch, Martha G. 56
  Mary M. H. 15
  Nancy C. 65

Lyons, Tabitha 97

-Mc-

McCaw, Martha 99
McKenney, Eliz. 66
  Mary 82
McKenny, Delila 121
  Dicey 120
  Eliz. H. 53
  Jane 134
  Sally 25
  Susanna 3
McKinney, Mary 17
  Sara 59
McKinny, Susanna 3

-M-

Mabry, Ann 48
  Dorothy 60
  Frances 56
Maclin,_____ 34
  Amey 20, 22
  Ann 26, 67
  Catherine 87
  Catherine A.(?) 119
  Charlotte P. 88
  Cleora 74
  Eliz. 44, 73, 76, 82
  Eliza 55
  Harriet D. 132
  Judah 79
  Judith 72
  Leah 135
  Lucy 69
  Martha 109
  Mary 22, 39
  Mary C. S. 44
  Mary E. 75
  Nancy 19
  Nancy W. 75
  Patsey 104
  Rebecca 87
  Sally 60
  Susan J. 75
  Susanna 33
  Tabitha 88
Maddox, Pheobe 136
Magee, Fanny 112
Maghe, Rebecca 54
Maitland, Agness S. 74
  Eliz. 76
  Mary Jane 74
Major, Ann 51, 52
  Eliz. 57
Mallory, Eliz. W. 116
  Lucy Ann 101
  Mary Jane 106
  Nancy 64
Malone, Amanda 83
  Ann 50
  Citivia 135
  Katherine 22
  Martha 102
  Mary 120
  Nancy 38
  Patsy 67
  Sally 16
  Sarah 121
  Wilmouth 120
Mangum, Julia 26

Mangum (cont.)
  Martha J. 38
  Rebecca 48
  Susan C. 74
Manly, Nancy 129
Mann, Catherine S. 131
Manning, Eliz. 19
  Lucy E. G. 101
  Margaret J. 84
  Mary 29
  Nancy 75
  Polly 18
  Sally 74, 133
Manson, Lucy F. 86
  Martha J. 76
  Mary Ann 122
  Mary B. 114
  Susanna 62
  Susanna H. 47
Mares, Eliz. 86
Marks, Nancy 85
  Polly B. 33
Marriott, Eliz. 101
  Hannah 28
  Sarah 56
Marshall, Patsy 83
Martin, Mary Ann 72
Mason, Ann E. 15
  Ann Eliza 128
  Eliz. 110
  Frances 7
  Indiana 111
  Louisa 16
  Margaret L. 127
  Martha 59, 66
  Martha J. 45
  Mary A. 78
  Mary M. 54
  Nanny 100
  Polly 48
  Sally 47
  Sarah 84
Massey, Delila 126
  Martha 81
  Sarah 61
Massie, Agness 100
  Amy 4
  Mary 132
  Rebecca 54
  Sarah 4
Mathews, Angelica 123
  Betsey 109
  Betsy 60
  Hannah 56
  Harriet 116
  Jincy 115
  Lucy 8
  Martha 106
  Maryland R. 106
  Nancy 33
  Polly 112
  Susanna A. 24
Mathis, Angelica Jones 77
  Anna 49
  Eliz. 37
  Mary 87
  Sarah 34
Matthews, Ann Eliza 73
  Eliz. 106
  Lucy 4
  Nelly 87
Mattocks,_____ 45
Mattox,_____ 50
  Mary 45
  Prudence 118
  Sarah 70
Mausback, Charlotte 106
Mayton, Martha 136

Meade, Amelia 40
  Ann 36, 53
  Harriett 105
  Maria 112
  Maria E. 38
  Marietta E. 11
  Matilda F. 128
  Susanna 37
Meanly (Manly?), Mary 78
Medlin, Anna 76
  Eliz. 69
Meredith, Ann 120
  Eliz. 102
  Martha 117
  Mary W. 8
  Nancy 97
  Sally 86
Merrit, Mary 33
Merritt, Eliz. 101
  Martha 34
  Mary 33
Meskell, Rebecca 42
Miller, Clarissa 37
  Julia Ann 17
  Mary 13
  Nancy 59
  Susanna 14
Miskell, Betsy H. 13
  Frances 81
  Winifred Beckwith 38
Mitchell, Ann 16
  Betty 49
  Eliz. 124
  Eliz. C. 81
  Eliz. H. 55
  Jane 4
  Lucy 85
  Martha Ann 115
  Mary 13, 72
  Rebecca 4
  Sally 29, 62
  Sarah P. 10
  Scoty 17
  Susan 129
  Tilly 89
Mize, Martha 80
  Mary F. 101
  Middy 79
  Rebecca 12
  Sarah 81
  Tabitha 10
Montgomery, Eliz. L. 120
Moody, Eliza A. 109
  Patsy 80
  Priscilla M. 97
Moore, Ann 79
  Ann E. 134
  Betsy 64
  Catherine E. 45
  Eliz. 23, 48
  Emmaline 36
  Fanny 68
  Frances 110
  Jane 104
  Louisa 134
  Marenda F. 105
  Margaret B. 71
  Martha 3, 96
  Martha Ann 19
  Martha E. 131
  Mary N. 35
  Pulcheria 34
  Rebecca 1
  Sally 36, 114
  Sarah J. 49
  Susan 1
Morris, A. B. 121
  Athelia 47

Morris (cont.)
  Claremon 43
  Eliz. 5, 117
  Julia 135
  Leicee 108
  M. A. J. 50
  Martha 4
  Martha L. 75
  Mildred 44
  Nancy 47
  Patsey 20
  Rebecca 82
  Sarah 17, 24
  Susanna(h) 23, 24
Morrison, Mary T. 75
Morriss, Frances 53
  Jincey 25
  Martha 22
  Rebecca 77
Morse, Almira L. 93
  Eliza 93
Moseley, Abby 56
  Amey 15, 69
  Ann 94
  Eliz. 17
  Huldah 46
  Mansfield 10
  Patsey 116
  Patsy 116
  Polly 106
  Rebecca 46, 122
  Rody 111
  Sally 68
  Sarah 21
  Thirza 68
Mosely, Nelly 82
  Tabitha 83
Moss, Arian S. 89
  Betty 62
  Eliz. 68
  Eliz. L. 133
  Lucreaty 86
  Mary J. 64
  Polly 91
  Sally 56
  Susanna 64
Murrell, Eliza 21
  Martha 132
  Nancy 90
Myrick, Ann 137
  Mary 33
  Middleton 37
  Sarah 125

-N-

Nance, Eliz. 39
  Mildred 30
  Sarah 67
Nanney, Frances 76
  Sylvanus 81
Nanny, Amey 100
  Caroline E. 116
  Eliz. 32
  Elvira 28
  Jensey 36
  Lydia 80
  Middy 128
  Molly 128
  Nancy 99
  Rebecca 126
  Rhoda 81
  Ritta 109
  Sarah 33
  Tabitha 13

147

Nanny (cont.)
  Winifred 13
Naper, Ann 57
Nash, Eliz. 56
  Eliz. A. 5
  Rebecca 25
Neal, Eliz. 45
  Joanna D. 108
  Mary 18
  Nancy 104
  Susan S. 92
Neale, Anny 21
Nevison, Ann 34
Newman, Emma A. 122
  Verenda S. 122
Newsom, Eliz. 10
  Susan M. 117
Newsum, Catherine 104
  Nancy 131
Nicholson, Eliz. 13, 127
  Sally 126
Nipper,_____ 102, 127
  Ann 37
  Nancy 6
Noble, Susanna S. 48
Nolley, Lucinda 112
  Mary 134
Nolly, Eliz. 102
  Lucy L. 39
  Susan J. 22
Norris, Sarah 85
Northington, Harriet R. 30
Nunnally, Jincy 68
  Lindy R. 72

-O-

Oast, Sary 66
Ogborn, Martha 114
Ogborne, Lucy 8
Ogburn, Eliz. 114, 120
  Eliza G. 58
  Harriet W. 24
  Lucy Ann 43
  Luch N. 108
  Martha E. 61
  Martha J. 130
  Mary 114
  Mary Jane 106
  Polly 97
  Sally 61
  Sarah W. 109
Oldham, Mary Ann 53
Oliver, Margaret 96
  Nancy 132
Orgain, Caroline M. 49
  Eliz. A. 107
  Eliz. S. 93
  Harriett M. 65
  Jane G. 93
  Lucy 1
  Mary W. 129
  Rebecca L. 86
  S. A. 27
  Susan G. 93
Orgean, Sally 90
Overby, Angelica 62
  Ann 42
  Eliz. 47
  Keziah 80
  Mary H. 116
  Nancy 116
  Patty 92

Owen, Elinor Hughes 35
  Eliz. J. 45
  Lucy S. 45
  Martha 66
  Mary 75
  Mary E. 45
  Nancy 52
  Sally 134
  Sarah A. 126
  Sydney J. 47
Owens, Lovey 108
  Nancy 134

-P-

Palmer, Ann M. 49
  Catherine E. 111
  Lucy W. 1
  Mary F. 122
Parham, Ann Eliza 77
  Eliz. 79
  Eliz. P. 48
  Frances 41, 56
  Mary 31
  Mary Ann C. 115
  Mary Branch 67
  Mary J. 15
  Nancy 16
  Obedience 63
  Rebecca 40, 55
  Sally P. 11
  Sarah 3, 4, 56, 95
  Susan 67, 95
  Tabitha 51
Parish, Eliz. 1
  Frances 31
  Julia A. 62
  Lucretia A. 63
  Martha K. 91
  Mary E. 52
  Sally E. 30
  Sarah 93
  Vincey 35
Parker, Eliz. 27, 66
  Martha 137
  Nancy 6
  Rebecca 130
Parrish, Jane 26
Parsons, Eliz. 80
  Mary 131
Patillo, Nancy 22
  Sally 70
Pattway, Ruth 108
Paup, Priscilla 12
  Sally P. 93
Payne, Eliz. 124
Pearcy, Ann 79
Pearson, Cesley 127
  Eliz. B. 89
  Lucy 117
  Martha 98
  Mary S. 105
  Midia 24
  Nancy 51, 71
  Patty 13
  Rebecca 125
  Tabitha 13
Peebles, Agness 93, 136
  Eliz. 16
  Eliza Jane 54
  Martha 30
  Mary 24, 67
  Mary D. 98
  Rebecca 10
  Sarah 61

Peebles (cont.0.
  Susan 106
Pegram, Susanna 3
Penn, Catherine 84
  Mary 69
  Nancy 62
  Sally 49
Pennington,_____ 16
  Ann 28
  Betsy 90
  Lucy 39
  Martha C. W. 81
  Martha J. 67
  Mary 36
  Sally 63
Pentecost, Peggy 104
Pepper, Eliz. 66
  Susanna 100
Percival, Eliz. 20
  Frances A. 70
  Margaret 64
  Rose Ann 11
Perkins, Ann C. 106
  L. Virginia 59
Perry, Jeanny 39
  Lucy 85
  Polly C. 115
  Priscilla 109
Person, Mary M. 134
Peterson, Frances 93
  Mary P. 38
  Susan 1
  Temperence 115
Pettaway, Martha Ann 1
Petillo, Lucy 34
  Mildred 65
  Rebecca 7
Pettit, Lucy 54
Pettway, Eliz. 133
  Lucretia 125
Petway, Cicely 74
  Lucy 9
Phenix, Cordelia 101
Pheonix, Eliz. 92
Philips, Polly 33
Phillips, Betsey 29
  Croline G. 130
  Patsy 62
  Prudence 79
  Sarah E. 65
  Sarah J. 130
Phillipson, Mary 136
Phipps, Adelaide W. 89
  Eliz. W. 17
  Mary 45
  Mary J. 63
  Mary S. 12
  Susan S. 63
Piercy, Eliz. 96
Pilkington, Betsy 63
Pincham, Mary 100
Pollard, Julia H. 4
Pool, Ann B. 28
Poole, Rebecca A. 88
Porch, Eliz. 124
  Susan 57
Porter, Lucy 29
  Nancy 12
  Polly 97
Potts, Eliz. 91
  Nancy 19
  Patsey 44
Powell, A. C. 135
  Ann S. 4
  Eliz. 17, 121
  Eliza M. 92
  Hannah E. 14
  Jane T. 86

Powell (cont.)
  Jean 54
  Jincy P. 57
  Lucy 9
  Lucy W. H. 63
  Martha A. 93
  Martha Ann 14
  Martha N. 86
  Martha T. 94
  Mary 111
  Nancy 84
  Polly 94
  Rebecca 44
  Rebecca G. 50
  Sally 93
  Sally H. 41
  Sarah Ann 7
  Tabitha 76
Powers, _____ 6
Poyner, Martha A. 122
  Mary W. 84
Preston, Anna 31
  Catherine S. 94
  Francis 111
  Martha 9
  Penelope 22
Price, Catherine 82
  Eliz. 30
  Mary E. 39
  Sylvia 49
Prior, Mary A. E. 60
Pritchett, Agness 102
  Agness C. 103
  Angelica M. 103
  Ann 93
  Anne E. 1
  Anne H. 22
  Eliz. 2
  Eliza M. 88
  Ermond 27
  Indiana J. C. 101
  Joanna H. 96
  Julia B. 28
  Julia E. 88
  Lucy 118
  Lucy A. L. 30
  Martha 63
  Martha A. 25
  Martha H. 60
  Martha M. 34
  Mary 27
  Mary L. 92
  Nancy 85
  Polly 34
  Sarah J. 27
  Sarah P. 103
  Susan W. 23
  Susanna 38
Proctor, Eliz. 8
  Katherine 102
  Priscilla 118
  Sarah 12
  Sucky 94
Pryor, Maria A. 124
  Susan C. 6
Purdy, Eliza 94

-Q-

Quarles, _____ 14
  Abel 117
  Ann 77
  Betsy 77, 118
  Caty 67, 131
  Mary 14

Quarles (cont.)
  Mary E. 45
  Nancy 77, 98
  Polly S. 118
  Sally Bell 117
  Susanna 12
  Quenshet(?), Sophia 120

-R-

Ragland, Macarina 3
Ragsdale, Nancy 37
  Susan A. E. 8
Raines, Eliza M. G. 44
  Hannah 108
  Lucy 108
Rainey, Eliz. 32, 116,
  136
  Mary 30
  Mary E. 18
Ramsay, Ruth 132
Randle, Ann 118
  Sausanna 57, 125
Randolph, Lucy B. 58
Ranson, Frances 92
Rash, Mary 6
Rawlings, Amanda G. 61
  Ann 46
  Ann E. 25
  Bromley 33
  Dolly 44
  Eliz. 23, 40
  Eliz. F. 115
  Eliza Ann 58
  Frances 114
  Hannah 43
  Henrietta 36
  Jane C. 43
  Lucy 43, 137
  Manerva J. 51
  Martha A. 97
  Martha D. 45
  Martha J. 43
  Mary 99
  Mary E. 48
  Nancy 33
  Nancy G. 42
  Polly 88
  Rebecca 39
  Sally 36
  Sally B. 5
  Susan 81
  Vicey 88
Ray, Amey 80
  Sally 98
Read, Ann 13
  Catherine 75, 95
  Eliz. 100
  Frances 113
  Jean 5
  Jemima 99
  Mynam 2
  Nancy 1, 6
  Olive 102
  Pharaby 46
  Polly 33
  Rebecca 18
  Silvey 42
  Susanna 59, 77
  Tabitha 8
  Winney 83
Read (Reid), Nancy 26
Reade, Eliz. 14
Redding, Rebecca 38
Reece, Ann 44

Reece (cont.)
  Betsey 92
  Mary 104
Reese, Susanna 14
Reid, Martha 60
Reives, Ann 90
  Betty 102
  Eliz. 76
  Julia 94
Rhea, Retta 18
Rhodes, Eliz. M. 4
  Phebe 97
Rice, Lucy A. E. 15
  Margaret 118
  Mary A. E. 50
  Mary Jones 60
  Peggy 121
  Rebecca 50
Richardson, Ann E. 75
  Frances 48
  Hannah H. 124
  Jane 18
  Lucy 41, 134
  Mary 102
  Sally 13
  Sarah 87
Rideout, Dolly 72
  Eliz. 66
  Jane 19
  Mary 7
  Minerva 88
  Sucky 121
Ridley, Louisa R. 137
Ridout, Frances 63
  Rebecca 107
Rivers, Ann 25
  Eliz. 7
  Hannah 81
  Martha 14
Rives, Ann E. 98
  Mary Chieves 38
  Tabitha 86
Roberts, Ann H. 84
  Patsy 41
  Polly 10
  Rebecca 127
Robertson, Ann E. 56
  Mary 19
  Rebecca 101
Robins, Lucy Jane 38
  Mary A. 62
  Susan M. 27
Robinson, Fanny 25
  Lucy 111
  Mary 91, 130
  Mary C. 129
  Polly 129
  Sally 101
Rogers, Delphia 107
  Eliz. 75
  Rebecca 85
  Susan 61
Rollings, Mary 7
Rose, Adelia L. 120
  Amey 129
  Eleann 118
  Lucy 106
  Martha E. C. 39
  Mary 103
  Rebecca 114
  Tabitha 28
  Theophane 106
Ross, Liddy 43
Rosser, Bathin 99
  Mary 28
Rowlett, Julia Ann 76
Russell, Ann 87
  Caty 65

Ryland, Eliz. J. 115
  Rebecca D. 42
  Sally 118

          -S-

Sadler, Eliz. 8
  Fanny 31
  Julia 131
  Mary 85
  Sophia 69
  Susan M. 110
Samford, Ann 98
  Eliz. 31, 104
  Hanna 58
  Jincy 65
  Mary 38, 82
  Sarah 107
  Virginia J. 4
Sammonds, Rebecca 43
Sammons, Fanny 113
Santy, Aggy 100
  Jinty 83
Saunders, Betsey 32
  Eliz. 30
  Frances P. 82
  Jensey 18
  Lucy 90
  Lucy M. 36
  Margaret 116
  Martha 67, 104
  Martha Ann 15
  Mary 39, 59
  Mary Ann 7
  Nancy 7
  Olive D. 100
  Rebecca 26
  Sarah J. 82
  Selah 67
  Sinah 17
Saxon, Temperance 92
Scarborough, Ann 95
  Eliz. 33
  Fanny 29
  Lucy 70
  Sally 48
Scarbrough, Martha 115
  Mary W. 14
  Rebecca 119
Scoggin, Eliz. 69
  Letitia 93
  Martha 103
  Martha E. 8
  Mary E. 14
  Pamelia Ann 34
  Rebecca 35
  Sarah 11
  Susanna 64
Scott, Amanda C. 112
  Lucy 94
Sealy, Judith 9
Seawell, Eliz. 72
  Mary 55
Seward, Ann E. 10
  Caty 80
  Charity 61
  Eliz. 13, 75
  Eliz. C. T. 110
  Fanny 85
  Lucetta Julia 46
  Lucy 126
  Margaret 125
  Martha 85
  Martha E. 16
  Martha G. 114

Seward (cont.)
  Nancy 32
  Patsey 33
  Polly 78
  Rebecca 16
  Sally 75
  Tabitha 12, 126
Sexton, Ann 78
  Mary 44
  Tabitha 110
Seymore, Ann E. 117
  Martha C. 73
Sharpe, Mary Ann 9
Shell, Ann E. 132
  Betsey 8
  Eliz. H. 11
  Martha 35
  Rebecca 19
  Theodicia 116
Shelton, Betty 102
  Harriet G. 77
  Jane 21
  Nancy 113
Short, ____ 1
  Clara 22
  Eliz. 74, 95, 112
  Eliz. M. 42
  Fanny 20
  Jean 119
  Lucy 64
  Mabel 106
  Margaret A. 76
  Martha 63
  Martha P. 71
  Mary 3, 91
  Mary A. E. 109
  Mary Jane 136
  Patty 64
  Rebecca 106
  Sally 9, 50
  Susan 59
  Susanna 22, 63
Sills, Martha Ann 42
  Sally 20
Simmons, ____ 32, 44, 87
  Ermine 32, 33
  Jane 15
  Lucy 60
  Martha 36, 39, 60
  Mary 118, 121
  Mason 82
  Sarah 53
  Susanna 33
  Vicy 113
Simms, Dorothy 122
  Mary 3
  Mary J. 5
  Susan S. 110
Sims, ____ 135
  Ann 117
  Eliz. 4, 45, 129
  Eliz. D. 61
  Martha 85
  Mary 97, 136
  Nancy 109
  Rebecca 128
  Rebecca W. 40
  Sally 117
  Tabitha 128
Singleton, Eliz. 18
  Frances 108
  Milly 116
  Nancy 18
  Rebecca C. 123
  Susanna 116
Sisson, Ann 47
  Eliz. 113
  Isabel 29

Sisson (cont.)
  Mary 29
  Skinner, Mary 124
  Slate, Eliz. 109
  Jane 89
  Mary 36
  Patsy 108
  Polly 44
Smiley, Ann S. 130
Smith, Ann 14, 28, 135
  Anna 24
  Cornelia A. 119
  Dousey 3
  Eliz. 83, 91, 94, 117
  Eliz. F. 16
  Eliz. S. 34
  Eliza 123, 134
  Emily A. 41
  Evelina 19
  Frances 55
  Frances H. 112
  Harriet 122
  Louisa A. 20
  Lucy Ann 107
  Lucy J. 103
  Maria F. 101
  Martha 40, 41
  Mary 57, 92, 107
  Mary Ann R. 33
  Mary H. 120
  Mary J. 74, 123
  Middy 124
  Mildred 26
  Nancy E. 89
  Nancy P. 133
  Olive H. 119
  Patsy 77
  Polly 25, 90
  Rebecca 71
  Sally R. 43
  Sarah 43, 110
  Susanna 84, 117
  Winny 124
Spain, Mary W. 112
Speake, Eliz. 131
Spears, Mary 79
Speed, Martha 67
Spicer, ____ 8
Spilman, Jenny 133
Stainback, Ann 47
  Ann E. 16
  Charlotte 106
  Eliz. 90, 91, 129
  Jane 57, 72
  Martha 33
  Mary 72, 86
  Patsey 42
  Rebecca 12, 132
  Rebecca J. 116
  Sally 44
  Sarah 32
  Susanna 52
Stanley, Sarah W. 26
Starback, Harriet 99
Starke, Dianotia Ravens-
    croft 59
  Eliz. 30
  Frances 58
Steed, Abigail 3
  Cresey 50
  Martha 83
  Mary A. 92
  Patsy 92
  Polly 128
  Priscilla H. 46
  Santhy C. 134
Stegall, Christian 37
  Dorcas 26

150

Stegall (cont.)
   Dorothy 84
   Eliz. 129
   Martha 121
   Mary E. 53
Stewart, Lucy 32
   Martha 75
   Nancy 99
   Rebecca 72
Stith, _____ 44
   Amanda M. 17
   Ann 31, 37
   Ann E. 42
   Ariana 125
   Charlotte E. 3
   Eliz. 101
   Eliz. B. 36
   Eliz. F. 136
   Eliz. J[ones] 119
   Eliza 132
   Eliza Caroline 85
   Frances 54
   Helen 40
   Julia B. 82
   Katherine 11, 113,
      128
   Louisa Ann 133
   Lucy 62
   Martha 36
   Martha A. E. 86
   Mary 36, 72
   Mary M. 92
   Minerva 58
   Rebecca 111
   Sarah W. 47
   Susan C. 26
   Susanna 78, 136
Stone, Caty 92
   Lucy Ann 74
   Sally Ann 1
Stradford, Ann 75
Strange, Eliz. 103
   Frances 130
   Mary 87
   Sarah 108
   Wilmouth 21
Stuart, Helen Wray 32
   Rebecca 19
Sturdivant, Althea 128
   Elvira 37
   Lucy 82
   Martha A. E. 119
   Mary Ann 49
   Nancy 113
Suggett, Rebecca 94
Sullivant, Joyce 99
Swanson, _____ 84
Sykes, Martha 86

                -T-

Talley, Betsy 102
   Eliz. M. 45
   Martha 66
   Mary Ann 40
Taney, Ann 61
Tarpley, Eliz. 97
   Martha 122
   Nancy Lewis 27
   Nancy W. 29
   Polly 108
   Sally W. 2
   Susan Ann 6
   Winifred 86
Tarver, Nancy 2

Tatum, Louisa H. 15
   Lucy 119
   Mareah 62
   Mary 33
   Rebecca 6, 70, 71
   Susanna 49
Taylor, Ann 63
   Jane 84
   Lucretia 3, 59
   Martha 118
   Martha A. 124
   Mary 137
   Nancy 105
   Nancy B. 21
   Patsy 83
   Polly 21, 117
   Rebecca 77
   Sally 5, 97, 115
   Sally A. 20
   Sally J. 107
   Susan 8, 133
Tazewell, Ann 84
Thacker, Bathsheba 116
Thomas, Cadijah 20
   Eliz. Huling 70
   Eliza A. 62
   Rebecca Ann 128
   Sarah F. 59
Thomason, Emily 65
   Ermine 39
   Faithy 115
   Mary 81
   Sally 36
Thommason, Harriet S.
   108
Thompson, Betsy 100
   Eliz. 82
   Eliz. B. 26
   Harriet J. 74
   Jane C. 26
   Mary 81
   Mary S. 120
   Polly 21, 109
   Sally 82
   Sarah M. 28
Thornton, Ann 86
   Jane 22, 56
   Mary 35
Threadgill, Eliz. 113
Thrift, Polly 70
Thrower, Ann C. 26
   Batty 38
   Eliz. 107
   Evalina H. 117
   Franky 105
   Lucinda 84
   Lucy 105
   Martha 41
   Minerva 114
   Rebecca 132
   Sally 2
   Sally S. 14
   Tabitha 35
Thweatt, Eliz. 9
   Jane 76
   Judith 40
   Martha T. 96
   Mary 15
   Patty 24
   Sarah 79
   Tabitha 43
Tillman, Mary 117
   Sarah 42
Tilly, Eliz. 29
Tilman, Eliz. 51, 93
   Lucy 88
   Martha 12
   Mary 25

Tinsbloom, Rebecca 126
Tomlinson, Eliz. 58
Traylor, Eliz. 78
   Martha 46
Trotter, Caty 114
   Eliz. 118
   Henrietta T. 78
   Jane 69
   Martha E. 4
   Martha L. 15
   Mary 55
   Mary Ann C. 51
   Nancy 76
   Susan J. 86
Tucker, Aphalia K. U. 100
   Elizabeth 11
   Lucy G. 19
   Margaret 126
   Martha W. 57
   Patsy C. 40
   Sarah M. 50
Tudor, Ann W. 88
Tuell, Tabitha 28
Turbeville, Dorothy K. 12
   Mary Ann 35
   Susan J. 46
Turbeyfield, Lucy 92
Turbyfield, Rebecca 39
Turbyfill, Harriet A.? 51
   Minerva O. 119
Turnbull, Ann A. 53
   Eliza J. 78
   Margaret S. 136
   Mary 17
   Mary C. 82
   Matilda C. 3
Turner, Betsy 106
   Burchet 41
   Dorcas 22
   Eliz. 55
   Hannah 19
   Martha 70
   Mary 15
   Priscilla 99, 100
   Sally 108
   Sarah 26
Twitty, Betty 20

                -U-V-

Underhill, Eliz. 39
   Julia A. G. 15
   Polly P. 104
Urvin, Amy 132
   Eliz. 55
Valentine, Martha 17
Vaughan, Amey 88
   Ann E. 121
   Beckey 127
   Caty 30
   Eliz. 74
   Eliz. A. 26
   Eliz. B. 17
   Frances 23
   Hannah 7, 92
   Harriet B. 126
   Julia 31
   Karen 10
   Lucy B. 14
   Lucy M. J. 119
   Martha 95, 123
   Mary M. 63
   Nancy 54
   Patience 4
   Peggy 125

Vaughan (cont.)
  Polly 7, 67, 103
  Rebecca E. H. 21
  Sally 50
  Sarah 120
  Sarah W. 122
  Silvey 88
  Sinah 9
  Susan 1
  Susanna 36
Vick, Catey 133
Vines, Dorothy 13

-W-

Wade, Eliz. 35
  Nancy 107
  Susanna 86
Walker, A. E. 34
  Betsy 38
  Cinthia J. 30
  Clancy 122
  Dicey 121
  Eliz. 66, 69, 98
  Eliz. Ann 64
  Eliz. H. 23
  Harriet 123
  Lucretia B. 111
  Lucy 27
  Lucy C. 73
  Mary 31
  Mary Ann 34
  Mary J. 2, 46
  Mary R. H. 55
  Nancy 73
  Polly 77
  Rebecca 29, 117
  Rebecca J. 108
  Sally A. 115
  Sarah E. 89
  Sarah S. 88
  Susanna 33
Wall, Eliz. 107
  Hannah 116
  Martha 116
  Mary 11
  Rebecca 76, 122
  Sally 9, 31
Wallace, Hannah 98
  Keziah 133
  Sally 18
Waller, Cresey 115
  Dolly 137
Wallon, Sally 29
Walpole, Faithy 123
  Jemima H. 17
  Nancy 120
  Sally 17
Walton, Catherine 49
  Eliz. 112, 124
  Lucretia 125
  Lucy P. 29
  Martha 41
  Martha J. 25
  Mary 68, 89, 92
  Mary Ann 6
  Matilda F. 56
  Nancy B. 131
  Nancy E. 41
  Patsey 66
  Phebe 120
  Rebecca 30, 109
  Sally 109
Ward, Eliz. 39
  Lucy 110

Ward (cont.)
  Mary 110
Warmock, Middy 89
Warren, _____ 49
  Eliz. 49, 66
  Hannah 85
  Martha 57
  Rebecca 47
  Rita 50
  Sarah 56
  Tempy 66
Warson, Eliz. J. 56
Warwick, Eliz. 40
  Eliza C. 52
  Margaret 135
  Polly 124
Washington, Ann 23
  Mary 57
  Rachel 137
Watson, Edith A. B. 89
  Eliz. 76
  Eliz. S. 124
  Lucretia 115
  Martha 72
  Mary 47
  Sally 24
Watts, Ann K. 41
  Mary L. 35
  Sarah L. 77
Weathers, Lucy 32
Weaver, _____ 53
  Agness A. 64
  Ann 64
  Betsey 61
  Betsy 60
  Eliz. 129
  Lucy M. 99
Webb, Eliz. 39, 65
  Martha J. 23
  Mary 10
  Mary E. 110
  Sarah A. 63
  Winifred 12
Weldon, Jane J. 137
  Mary E. 137
Wells, Jane E. 58
  Julian 59
Wesson, Betsy 86
  Dicey 122
  Eliz. 61
  Eliz. C. 105
  Evelina T. 46
  Frances 125
  Jane 95
  Jincy 126
  Keziah 45
  Lucy 127
  Lucy L. 126
  Martha 21
  Martha J. 126
  Martha W. 47
  Mary 62
  Mary J. 42
  Sally 134
  Susan 80
  Tempy 131
West, Lucy 99
Westmoreland, Ann 52
  Betsy 71
  Hummons 67
  Martha P. 26
  Rebecca 96
  Ruth 96
  Susanna 52
Wheeler, Eliz. 133
  Frances 72
  Lucy 82
  Milly 58

Wheeler (cont.)
  Susanna 13
Whett, Polly 88
Whitby, Mary Olive 51
White, Catherine E. 34
  Clementine Carter 11
  Eliz. 51
  Eliz. A. 83
  Hannah 42
  Lucy 115
  Rebecca 95
  Rebecca C. 56
  Sarah 10, 46, 79, 116
Whitechurch, Eliz. 9
Whitehead, Eliz. 118
  Mary 22
Whitfield, Jean 69
Whitington, Rebecca 125
Whitlock, Eliz. 72
Wilburn, Lucy 90
Wilkerson, Ann 66
Wilkes, Ann 86
  Eliz. 21
  Eliz. J. 134
  Frances 7
  Julia G. 97
  Lucretia A. 36
  Margaret W. W. 88
  Martha J. 90
  Mary B. 30
  Mary G. 67
  Miner 97
  Susan 96
  Susan C. 96
Wilkinson, Ann C. 57
Williams, Amy 57
  Ann 52, 59
  Ann J. 46
  Betsey 32
  Betsy 103, 110, 122
  Charlotte 32
  Eliz. 48, 61, 129
  Eliz. E. 105
  Eliza 28
  Francis 49
  Henrietta C. 131
  Jane C. 74
  Jincy 126
  Lucy 19, 127
  Lucy M. 117
  Lucy R. 124
  Martha 8, 88, 91, 95, 119
  Martha A. 85
  Mary 22, 75, 92
  Mary A. J. 111
  Milly B. 54
  Nancy 87, 115, 120
  Patsey 124
  Polly 88, 90, 131
  Rachel 54, 56
  Rebecca 2, 52
  Rhody 62
  Sally A. 60
  Sarah 56, 92, 130
  Sarah D. 102
  Su. E. 53
  Susan 104
  Susan T. 6
  Tabitha 72, 79
  Winifred 96
Williamson, Ann 137
  Edith 68
  Eliz. 113, 119
  Hannah 38, 118
  Martha 19
  Milly 99
  Sally 24
  Sarah 73

152

Williamson (cont.)
  Susanna 102
Willis, Eliz. 22
Wills, Anney 21
Wilson, Betsy 66
  Mary 84
  Nancy 95
  Pamela S. 101
  Patsy 102
  Polly 67
  Sally Baugh 75
  Sarah B. 62
  Susan G. 21
  Winifred 135
Wiltshire, Milly 65
Winfield, Martha 122
  Mary 61
  Sally 20
  Sarah Ann 97
Wingfield, Eliz. 78
Winn, Ann E. 65
  Clara 69
  Eliz. 100
  Martha A.? 31
  Mary H. 31
  Susan J. 106
Woodlief, Elvira 136
Woodroff, Sally 52
Woodrough, Jane 48
  Mary 72
Woodruff, Martha 62
  Mary 121
  Nancy P. 80
  Rebecca 100
Woolsey, Ann 84
  Mary E. 55
  Polly 131
  Sally 29
  Tabitha 124
Worthington, Caroline 21
  Eliza 60
  Frances J. 115
  Sarah 39
Wray, Betsy 69
  Eliz. W. 71
  Eliza Jane 74
  Martha 68
  Nancy 134
  Nelly 62
  Patsy 39
  Rebecca 17
  Sinthey 45
  Susan 131
  Tempy 18
Wrenn, Polly 93
Wright, Armantena 134
  Dicey 68
  Eliz. 99
  Elsey 65
  Lucy 87
  Mary 83
  Nancy 58, 69
  Nelly 98
  Rachel 32
  Rebecca 89
  Sally 49, 127, 134
Wyall, Agness B. 36
Wyatt, Ann C. 36
  Frances 130
  Mary 53, 120
  Mary Ann 12
Wyche, Abigail 13
  Betsy 102
  Lucy G. 125
  Polly 35
  Rebecca 70
  Sally 98
  Tabitha 19

Wynn, Ann E. W. 84
Wynne, Betty 133
  Henrietta S. 123
  Marticia 10
  Nancy 53
  Patsy 85
  Patty Jones 76
  Polly 77, 105, 136
  Sally 85
  Susan 53

          -Y-Z-

Yeargin, Eliz. 99
Zachry, Sally 102
Zimmer, Antionette 106

9 780806 307046